2016

Paper 3 – Issues and Option 1 Cognition & Development

Nick & Bethan Redshaw

The Independent Learner Series

The Independent Learner Series

A-Level Psychology

Paper 3: Issues and Option 1 Cognition and Development

2016

© Advanced Success Ltd

ISBN: 978-1-326-80866-2

Table of Contents

Ten Good Reasons...
To Study Psychology

1. Studying psychology will help you to gain a better understanding of your own behaviour as well as that of other people . . .

School, sports, employment, health, business, marriage, being young, growing older . .

Each aspect of our lives is touched by how we think, behave and respond . . . The way we eat, how we sleep, how we express ourselves; the things that make us feel energetic or feel happy; the situations that make us feel sad or angry . . .

It's all controlled by aspects of **Human Psychology!**

2. It will equip you with a wide range of scientific, social and essay writing skills

3. You will learn how psychologists conduct experiments and research so that their work is both scientific and credible

4. You will analyse and examine major controversies in psychology including moral and ethical issues

5. An initial A-level will give you a good head start if you want to study Psychology at university

6. Psychology will enhance many other areas of your study including law, sociology, biology, criminology, literature, writing, business, sports, drama . . .

7. You will learn to manage your own time and study progress through independent study - universities and employers will recognise and respect your personal commitment

8. Throughout the course you will be able to develop your skills in self motivation, reading, writing, evaluation, analysis, research and communication

9. These valuable skills are highly regarded by employers and are transferrable to many different career paths

10. The future is YOURS!!! Learning about psychology is a good way of helping yourself toward a confident and successful future

Specification at a glance

This qualification is linear. Linear means that you will sit all the exams at the end of your A Level course.

Subject Content

This workbook covers the Compulsory Content for Paper 3 Issues and Debates and your chosen topic from Option 1 only. To successfully complete Paper 3 you will also need to purchase additional workbooks from our series to cover the one topic you have chosen from Option 2 and Option 3.

Assessments

Paper 1: Introductory topics in psychology	+	Paper 2: Psychology in context	+	Paper 3: Issues and options in psychology
What's assessed Compulsory content 1–4 above		**What's assessed** Compulsory content 5–7		**What's assessed** Compulsory content Issues and Debates and three Optional content, one from: option 1: 9–11 option 2: 12–14 option 3: 15–17
Assessed • written exam: 2 hours • 96 marks in total • 33.3% of A-level		**Assessed** • written exam: 2 hours • 96 marks in total • 33.3% of A-level		**Assessed** • written exam: 2 hours • 96 marks in total • 33.3% of A-level
Questions Section A,B,C and D Multiple choice, short answer and extended writing, 24 marks		**Questions** Section A,B,C and D Multiple choice, short answer and extended writing, 24 marks		**Questions** Section A,B,C and D Multiple choice, short answer and extended writing, 24 marks

Paper 3 Issues and Option 1 Cognition and Development

This workbook covers the optional content you need for the exam, no prior knowledge is needed, however, most schools and independent students start with Paper 2 as it covers research methods and ethics which are needed throughout the specific content for Paper 1, 2 and 3 and throughout your course you are expected to:

- demonstrate and apply knowledge and understanding of psychological concepts, theories, research studies, research methods and ethical issues in relation to the specified Paper 3 content in a range of contexts
- analyse, interpret and evaluate psychological concepts, theories, research studies and research methods in relation to the specified Paper 3 content
- evaluate therapies and treatments including in terms of their appropriateness and effectiveness.

Knowledge and understanding of research methods, practical research skills and mathematical skills will be assessed in Paper 3. These skills should be developed through study of the specification content and through ethical practical research activities, involving:

- designing research
- conducting research
- analysing and interpreting data.

In carrying out practical research activities, you will be expected to manage associated risks and use information and communication technology (ICT)

Issues and Debates in Psychology	Green	Amber	Red
1. Gender and culture in psychology – universality and bias. Gender bias including androcentrism and alpha and beta bias; cultural bias, including ethnocentrism and cultural relativism.			
2. Free will and determinism: hard determinism and soft determinism; biological, environmental and psychic determinism. The scientific emphasis on causal explanations.			
3. The nature-nurture debate: the relative importance of heredity and environment in determining behaviour; the interactionist approach.			
4. Holism and reductionism: levels of explanation in psychology. Biological reductionism and environmental (stimulus-response) reductionism.			
5. Idiographic and nomothetic approaches to psychological investigation.			
6. Ethical implications of research studies and theory, including reference to social sensitivity.			

Option 1 – Cognition & Development	Green	Amber	Red
1. Piaget's theory of cognitive development: schemas, assimilation, accommodation, equilibration, stages of intellectual development. Characteristics of these stages, including object permanence, conservation, egocentrism and class inclusion.			
2. Vygotsky's theory of cognitive development, including the zone of proximal development and scaffolding.			
3. Baillargeon's explanation of early infant abilities, including knowledge of the physical world; violation of expectation research.			
4. The development of social cognition: Selman's levels of perspective-taking; theory of mind, including theory of mind as an explanation for autism; the Sally-Anne study. The role of the mirror neuron system in social cognition..			

Issues and Debates

Learning Objectives

On completion of this unit you should be familiar with the following:

- Gender and cultural bias in psychology
- Ethical implications of research studies and theory
- Free will and determinism
- Idiographic and nomothetic approaches to psychological investigation.
- The nature-nurture debate
- Holism and reductionism

This unit looks at some of the main philosophical issues and debates in psychology in detail. You have been introduced to most of these issues and debates throughout the course as you will be expected, when answering questions in the exam, to demonstrate your knowledge and understanding of how they have shaped research and topics in psychology.

All the research, theories and approaches that you look at in psychology have their strengths and limitations and the ability to evaluate these effectively is crucial in the development of your knowledge and understanding of human behaviour.

To get you thinking about the different issues and debates in psychology – complete the table below using your previous knowledge of the approaches and give an example of an issue from each area.

Approaches	Gender Bias	Cultural Bias	Methodology	Ethical Issue
Learning Approaches				
Cognitive Approach				
Biological Approach				Animal Research
Psychodynamic Approach	Moral Dilemmas'			
Humanistic Psychology				

In the table below, give an one example of a theory, research or concept from a topic that might be considered to have issues of – gender bias, cultural bias or methodological and ethical issues.

Topic	Gender Bias	Cultural Bias	Methodological	Ethical Issues
Memory				
Attachment	Bowlby – Women need to stay at home and look after their children			
Social Influence			Zimbardo – taking part in own study researcher bias	
Psychopathology				
Biopsychology				

Issues in Psychology

Learning Objectives

On completion of this section you should be familiar with the following:

1. Universality and bias. Gender bias including androcentrism and alpha and beta bias.
2. Cultural bias, including ethnocentrism and cultural relativism.
3. Ethical implications of research studies and theory, including reference to social sensitivity.

Research should try to maintain an unbiased, factual, value-free position. This enables any conclusions that are drawn to be universally applied to all individuals regardless of gender or culture. However, this is rarely the case as pre-conceived values and judgments have a tendency to distort our attitudes and beliefs through schemas and stereotypes. Therefore, research is often subject to bias in favour of one gender or culture.

Outline the difference between universality and bias in psychological research.

....

....

....

....

....

....

....

(2 marks)

Schemas and stereotypes help us to make less biased conclusions. True or False?

True ☐   False ☐

(1 mark)

1. Gender bias including androcentrism and alpha and beta bias

Much of the research in psychology can be criticised for having an andro (male) centric (centred) bias. Many of the early psychologists were male, using experimental methods such as lab experiments which are regarded as having a male bias, used male participants and researched male topics such as obedience and conformity. Findings from these studies were used to universally explain behaviour in both sexes, when in fact they had no evidence to suggest women would act in the same way as men.

In addition, psychological theories portray women as inferior or morally deviant, compared to men, often exaggerating gender differences and reinforcing gender stereotypes. For example, men hunt women sew or women are more emotional than men. As a result, the findings of many research studies are gender biased and have led to misperceptions about women. Hare-Mustin and Maracek (1988) considered the issue of gender bias in psychological literature in detail and distinguished between two theoretical types of gender bias:

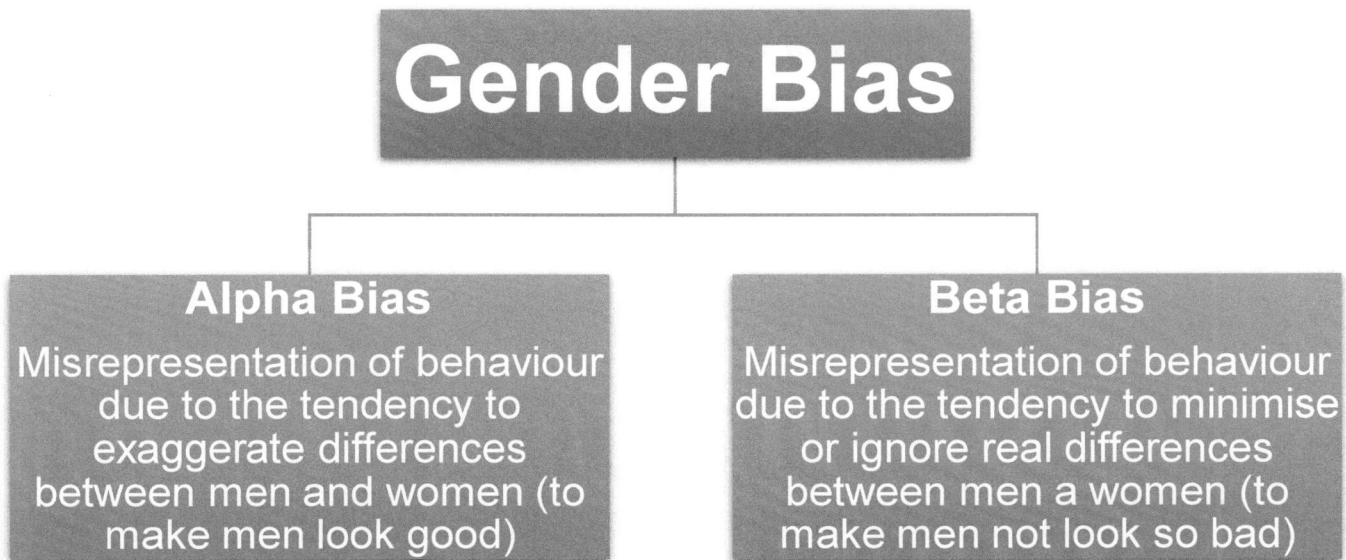

Gender Bias

Alpha Bias
Misrepresentation of behaviour due to the tendency to exaggerate differences between men and women (to make men look good)

Beta Bias
Misrepresentation of behaviour due to the tendency to minimise or ignore real differences between men a women (to make men not look so bad)

Briefly outline what psychologists mean by the term androcentric bias.

....

....

....

....

(2 marks)

Briefly outline one problem associated with alpha bias in psychological research, and one problem associated with beta bias in psychological research.

....

....

....

....

....

....

....

....

....

....

....

....

....

(4 marks)

Which of the following statements (A – D) about gender bias are true. Circle the two correct answers.

A   Alpha bias is the tendency to exaggerate gender differences

B   Beta bias is the tendency to exaggerate gender differences

C   Alpha bias is the tendency to minimise or ignore gender differences

D   Beta bias is the tendency to minimise or ignore gender differences

(2 marks)

Examples of Alpha Bias in Psychology

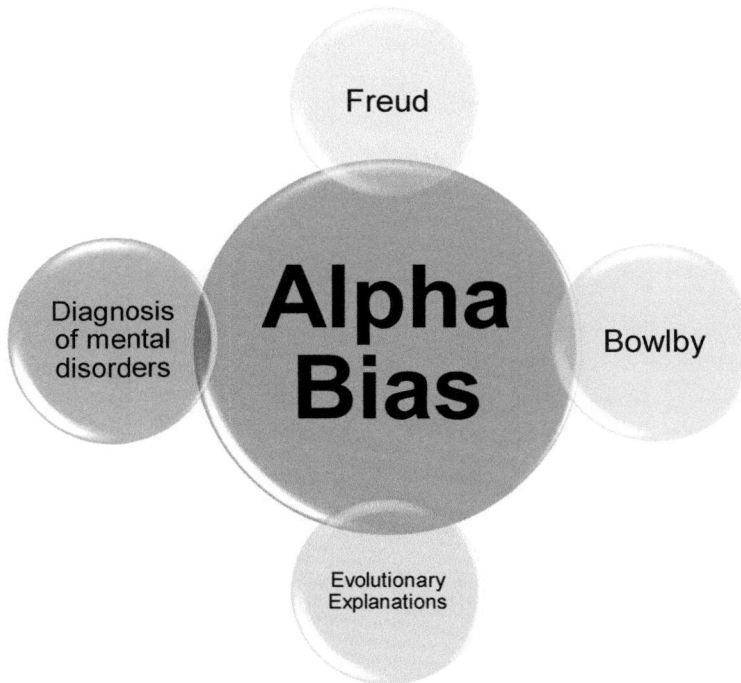

Freud argued that in through the Oedipus Complex boys develop a strong superego, as they identify with their father as they fear castration if they do not regulate their sexual desire towards their mother. According to Freud, girls do not develop such a strong superego as they blame their mother for castrating them and have penis envy, leading them to have a greater identification with their father. Such claims lead to the idea that women are inferior to men as they less morally developed than men, so exaggerating a difference between the sexes.

Bowlby's claim that women needed to stay at home and care for their children or else they would damage their children's social, cognitive and emotional development, implies that only the mother can fulfill this role. Therefore, reinforcing gender stereotypes.

According to evolutionary theories, men are portrayed as more dominant than females, women have a greater parental investment and men are more likely to commit adultery. Buss (1989) carried out a large cross-cultural study and found that men value physical attraction while women look for security and stability.

Hare-Mustin and Maracek (1988) claim that much of the research and literature used in the DSM and ICD classifications to diagnose depression were written by male doctors and psychologists and they have found that psychiatrists are more likely to diagnose depression in women compared with men, even when they have similar scores on standardised measures of depression or present with identical symptoms. In addition, women are more open about their problems and are more likely to visit the doctor for treatment. However, just because males do not report their symptoms does not mean they are not suffering from depression. Therefore, differences between the sexes are exaggerated.

Outline and evaluate the alpha bias issue in psychology.

....

....

....

....

....

....

....

....

....

....

....

....

....

....

....

....

....

....

....

....

....

....

....

....

....

....

....

....

....

....

....

....

....

....

....

....

....

....

....

....

....

....

....

....

(8 marks)

Examples of Beta Bias in Psychology

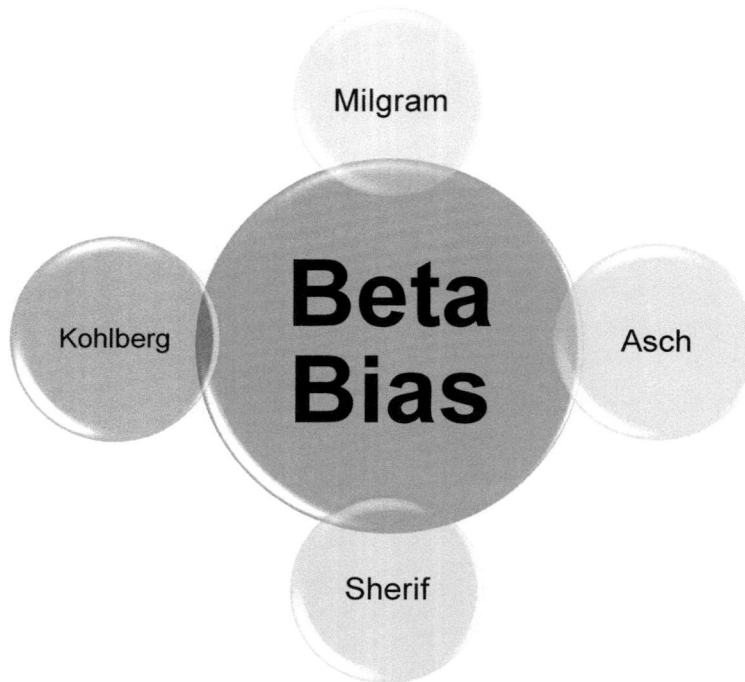

Kohlberg's (1963) Theory of Moral Development used research based mainly on male orientated dilemmas, and only used male participants. He assumed that there was minimal difference between men and women in terms of moral thinking, therefore it would not matter if he only used male participants.

Gilligan (1982) argued that Kohlberg's theory overemphasises the concept of justice when making moral choices. Other factors such as compassion, caring, and other interpersonal feelings may play an important part in moral reasoning, which females have a greater tendency towards. Therefore, Kohlberg's theory is beta biased as it minimises the difference in moral thinking between men and women.

Many of the research studies into social influence can be criticised for being beta biased. Discuss how Milgram, Asch and Sherif's research is beta biased.

....

....

....

....

....

....

....

....

....

....

....
....
....
....
....
....
....
....
....
....
....
....
....
....
....
....
....
....
....
....
....
....

(8 mark)

Maccoby and Jacklin (1974) carried out a review of psychological research and concluded that in the majority of areas there was no significant difference between men and women. So clearly the differences found are due to methodological issues within the research studies. Concerns regarding gender bias in psychology research have highlighted that the design of research can bias the chances of obtaining a particular finding and that this can lead to findings that lack validity. So, using same sex participants, choosing a particular research method (lab experiment), using a specific measure of behaviour (moral dilemmas) are examples of poor methodological constructs that lead to gender bias.

Reporting and publishing research which claims that one sex is better than the other (Freud) or that there is no difference between the sexes (Milgram) when their research has only focused on a limited sample is an example of reporting bias, leading to gender bias. A failure on behalf of the researcher to recognise these concerns or to take steps to ensure that these concerns are addressed or a particular motivation to achieve a certain outcome is researcher bias. According to feminist psychologists any gender differences are often minimal, however, they have often been used against women to subordinate them and reinforce gender stereotypes. Critics such as Bem (1994) have argued that in a male-centred world, female differences are viewed as female disadvantages, lowering their self-esteem and putting them under pressure to improve themselves.

Although there is evidence of gender bias within psychology, this is mainly based on historical research studies and theories that were constructed over 50 years ago. This section is designed to make you aware of these problems and give you the skills to ensure that you avoid gender bias in the design and conduct of your research and be able to identify examples of gender bias in the research of others.

Rosenthal (1966) stated that it is possible that sex differences are found in psychological research because researchers ignore the differential treatment of participants. Male experimenters may treat their female participants differently from their male ones.

Outline how a researcher may treat female participants differently to male participants and explain how they could deal with this issue.

....

....

....

....

....

....

....

....

(4 marks)

Gilligan (1982) argued that Kohlberg's Theory of Moral Development focused more on the concept of justice in the dilemmas, making the research androcentric.

Outline how you would design a measure of moral development that is not gender specific?

....

....

....

....

....

....

....

....

....

....

(4 marks)

Using same sex participants is good practice in psychological research. True or False?

True ☐ False ☐

(1 mark)

Which of the following statements (A – D) about gender bias are true. Circle the two correct answers.

A   Gender differences have been used to reinforce gender stereotypes

B   Gender bias is more of an issue today than 50 years ago

C   Gender differences are often minimal

D   Using lab experiments reduces gender bias

(2 marks)

2. Cultural bias, including ethnocentrism and cultural relativism

As we have already discussed, research should try to maintain an unbiased, factual, value-free position. In the previous section we looked at gender bias and in this section we will look at how our cultural values, attitudes, cultural perspectives, beliefs and ethnic backgrounds lead to cultural bias, through ethnocentrism and cultural relativism.

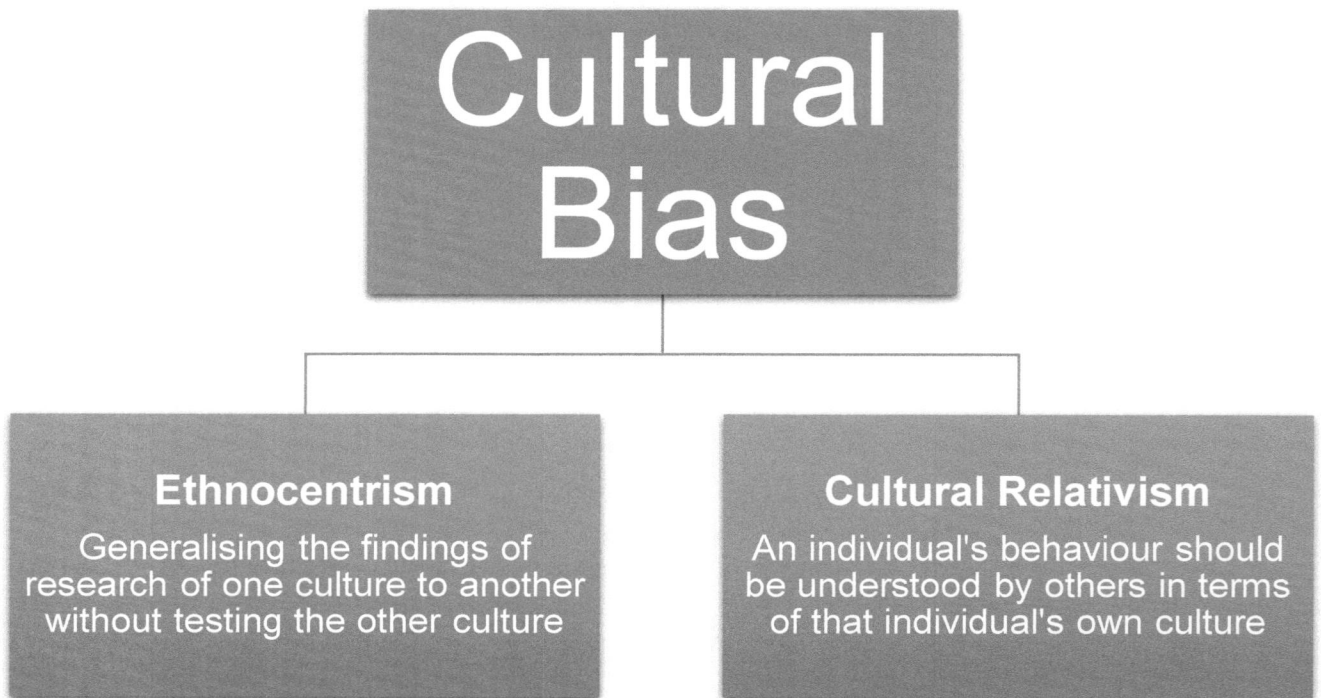

Cultural Bias

Ethnocentrism
Generalising the findings of research of one culture to another without testing the other culture

Cultural Relativism
An individual's behaviour should be understood by others in terms of that individual's own culture

Outline the difference between ethnocentrism and cultural relativism.

....

....

....

....

....

....

....

(2 marks)

Examples of Cultural Bias in Psychology

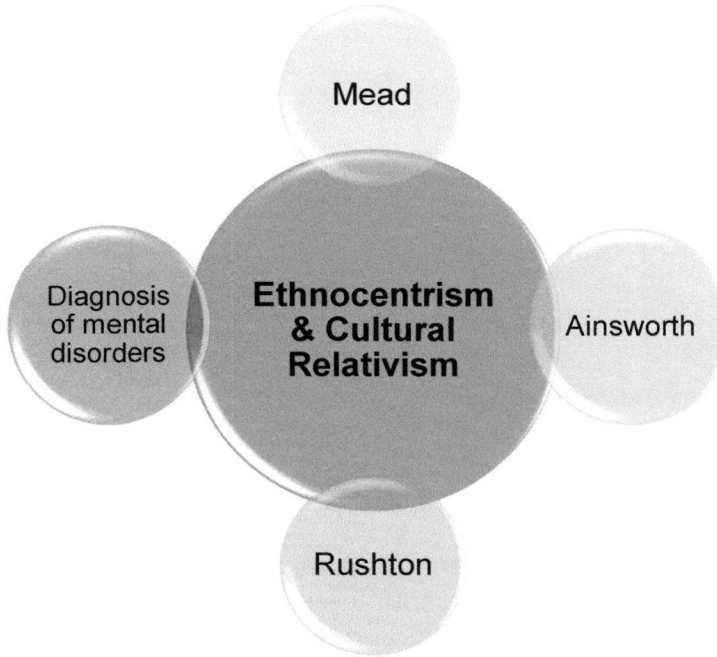

Mead

Diagnosis of mental disorders

Ethnocentrism & Cultural Relativism

Ainsworth

Rushton

Many psychological studies can be criticised for being culturally biased as they only use participants from one particular cultural background i.e. white Americans. Believing that universal factors hold true across all cultures, is known as an **etic construct**.

In addition, constructing research using the values and beliefs of one culture and use it to test another culture without taking into account any differences, is known as an **imposed etic.**

This would clearly lead to cultural bias. To prevent this the only true ecologically valid research would be that constructed from the perspective of the culture being studied, this approach would be known as an **emic construct**. Emic constructs recognise that cultures vary in terms of the above values and such designs provide far more ecologically valid findings.

Key Term

Emic Constructs
A test that is created and tested in one country, meaning that its construct may only reflect the norms and values of that culture

Imposed Etic
Imposing the judgements and values of one culture onto another

Etic Construct
Believing that universal factors hold true across all cultures

Briefly explain why using Ainsworth's strange situation technique to study cross cultural differences in attachment is criticised as being an imposed etic.

....

....

....

....

....

....

....

(2 marks)

Outline the difference between an emic construct and an etic construct.

....

....

....

....

....

....

....

(2 marks)

Like the research into cross-cultural differences in attachment there are issues with using a test designed in one country to diagnose mental disorders in other countries. As American and western cultural ideals have shaped the construction of both DSM-5 and ICD 10, they are both **emic constructs**. However, DSM-5 and ICD 10 assumes that there is no difference between cultures, so it is an **etic construct.** Therefore, when they are used to classify and diagnose phobias in non-western cultures they are an **imposed etic** and may not be measuring what they claim to be measuring.

Therefore, it is ethnocentrically biased and lacks cultural relativism. As a result of this, using DSM-5 and ICD 10 as a global diagnostic tool lacks validity i.e. it fails to diagnose what it is supposed to be diagnosing and it also fails to achieve the same results in different cultures, so it lacks reliability.

Complete the following sentence. Tick all boxes that apply.

It is claimed that the classifications of DSM-5 are ethnocentric because:

☐ A It place the judgements and values of one culture onto another

☐ B They are based on research carried out by male psychologists

☐ C It assumes that there is no difference between cultures

(1 mark)

Another type of ethnocentrism is racial bias, where much research over the years has focused on looking at differences between different ethnic groups. For example, a study carried out in America by Rushton (1988) reported that there was a significant difference between the IQ scores of white American and black African children. Rushton claimed that the test used was "culture free", however, it was heavily maths biased and favoured the white American children school children over the African children who had not received any schooling.

Explain how Rushton's research is culturally biased and outline the wider implications of his findings.

....

....

....

....

....

....

....

....

....

....

....

....

....

....

....

....

....

....

....

....

....

....

(6 marks)

A classic study carried out into gender development by Margaret Mead (1928) highlights the issue of cultural relativism and the need to judge an individual's behaviour in terms of that individual's own culture. Mead carried out a study of Samoan women as they developed from childhood through to adulthood to determine whether or not the problems associated with adolescence were due to nature or nurture. She found that the transition in Samoan women was not marked by the emotional or psychological distress, anxiety or confusion experienced by women in the United States. She concluded that the problems experienced in adolescence are socially constructed in Western society.

Mead's conclusions were sound, however, she also reported that young Samoan women deferred marriage for many years while enjoying casual sex but eventually married, settled down, and successfully reared their own children. This upset and shocked many Westerners when the report first published and made the Samoans look morally deviant.

In 1983, five years after Mead had died, Freeman challenged all of Mead's major findings. He argued that Mead had not spent enough time with the Samoan people to gain their trust and as a result they had only told her what they thought she wanted to hear and she had only seen what she had wanted to see. Therefore, her findings and conclusions lacked cultural relativism as they were based on her own values and beliefs.

Outline how Mead's study demonstrates cultural bias.

....

....

....

....

....

....

....

....

....

....

....

(4 marks)

3. Ethical implications of research studies and theory, including reference to social sensitivity.

The British Psychological Society (BPS) **code of ethics** maintains that all psychological research should be carried out in line with the four main ethical principles:

Respect
Statement of values – Psychologists value the dignity and worth of all persons, with sensitivity to the dynamics of perceived authority or influence over clients, and with particular regard to people's rights including those of privacy and self determination.

Competence
Statement of values – Psychologists value the continuing development and maintenance of high standards of competence in their professional work, and the importance of preserving their ability to function optimally within the recognised limits of their knowledge, skill, training, education, and experience.

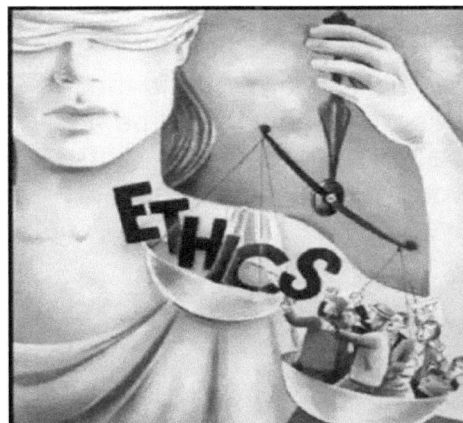

Responsibility
Statement of values – Psychologists value their responsibilities to clients, to the general public, and to the profession and science of Psychology, including the avoidance of harm and the prevention of misuse or abuse of their contributions to society.

Integrity
Statement of values – Psychologists value honesty, accuracy, clarity, and fairness in their interactions with all persons, and seek to promote integrity in all facets of their scientific and professional endeavours.

The code of ethics are a framework of how to carry out research, however, the reality of psychological research leads to a conflict between the ethical guidelines and the goal of the research study.

The four main issues that psychologists face are:

Definition	Guideline	Ethical Issues
Deception		
Deliberately withholding information that might affect the participant's decision to take part in the research	Deception of the participants during the research process should be avoided wherever possible	Withholding of the research hypothesis is often considered necessary in order to avoid demand characteristics

Informed Consent		
Participants should be made aware of any tasks required of them; their right to withdraw and any other aspects of the research that might affect their willingness to participate	Participants' agreement to take part in research should be based on their full knowledge of the nature and purpose of the research. When dealing with children under 16, parent or guardian permission needs to be given	Informed consent cannot be given as in doing so participants would be aware of the research hypothesis which would influence their behaviour (demand characteristics)

Protection from harm		
The risk of harm during the research study should be no greater than the participants would experience in their everyday life	The guideline states that participants should be protected from physical and psychological harm, such as distress, ridicule, or loss of self-esteem	In order for research to be realistic some distress may need to be caused to the participants.

Privacy and Confidentiality		
Participants in psychological research have a right to expect that information they provide will be treated confidentially and, if published, will not be identifiable as theirs	Information obtained about a participant during an investigation is confidential unless otherwise agreed in advance	During research participant may disclose information that is illegal or threatens their safety

Name and briefly outline two of the four principles of the BPS code of ethics in psychological research

....

....

....

....

....

....

....

....

(4 marks)

The BPS code of ethics is not a legal document but is a professional standard that all psychologists should adhere to when conducting psychological studies. It recognises that the ethical issues mentioned earlier will inevitably arise during the course of a psychologist's professional work and highlights that it is the researcher's responsibility to ensure that they have the professional competence and experience to deal with these ethical issues appropriately. In dealing with an issue a psychologist should seek guidance from others in the form of a peer review or ethical committee and reflect on their own practice at regular intervals.

Having done all this, the question that psychologists face is whether their research will require them to break the ethical guidelines and what the consequences of doing so will be. This is known as the cost-benefit analysis. If they decide to proceed with the research and it breaches the guidelines psychologists should deal with the ethical issues as follows:

Debriefing

One of the main reasons why a researcher cannot get informed consent is because of the need for deception. To deal with this the researcher will need to debrief the participants at the end of the investigation and t the true nature and purpose of the research is explained to the participants, which covers the fact that they were deceived and did not give their full consent. Debriefing is also used to reassure participants that their behaviour is normal and to address any distress caused by the research, thereby protecting the participants from harm.

The right to withdraw

To protect the participants from harm they are informed at the beginning of the research that if they are distressed or upset at any point they have the right to withdraw. It is also the responsibility of the researcher to stop the experiment if the participant becomes too distressed. The right to withdraw can also be used if the psychologist has failed to gain informed consent at the beginning of the study during the debrief participants are given the opportunity to withdraw their data if they are not happy.

Obtaining consent

Psychologists can obtain participant consent in three ways:

Prior general consent	Presumptive consent	Retrospective consent
Participants have already consented to take part in several different studies, so it is assumed that they will consent to the new research	The researcher has asked similar people if they would consent to the new research, if the agree then it is presumed that the participants will also consent	During the debriefing the participants are asked for their consent having already taken part in the new research

Privacy and Confidentiality

In order to ensure that a participant's data is kept confidential the psychologist should ensure that they record no personal details and maintain the anonymity of the participants at all times. This is usually achieved by numbering the participant or using letters such as HM or KF. If a participant discloses any information that the psychologist believes to be illegal or threatens the safety of the participant or others, the participant must be informed that they need to seek professional help or that the information will be passed on to the relevant authorities.

The ethics of socially sensitive research

Many of the studies we have looked at throughout this course have wider implications for those who are studied and society as a whole. Socially Sensitive research is any research that produces results that may cause people real or perceived problems, such as discrimination. For example, Rushton and Mead's studies discriminated against one race or culture. Sieber and Stanley (1988) and Lee (1993) state that all research has the potential to shape policy, so any research that is socially sensitive poses a greater threat or risk.

The BPS acknowledges that it can be difficult to determine all potential risks before research is carried out, but would normally be dealt with through the guidelines and code of ethics outlined in the previous section. However, there are some areas within psychology that the BPS consider as involving **more than minimal risk.** These include:

- Research involving vulnerable groups (such as children under 16; those lacking capacity; or individuals in a dependent or unequal relationship);
- Research involving potentially sensitive topics (such as sexual behaviour; political behaviour; their experience of violence; their gender or ethnic status);
- Research involving a significant and necessary element of deception;
- Research involving access to records of personal or confidential information
- Research involving access to potentially sensitive data through third parties
- Research involving invasive interventions (such as the administration of drugs or other substances, vigorous physical exercise or techniques such as hypnosis) that would not usually be encountered during everyday life;
- Research that may have an adverse impact on employment or social standing (e.g. discussion of an employer, discussion of commercially sensitive information);
- Research that may lead to 'labelling' either by the researcher (e.g. categorisation) or by the participant (e.g. 'I am stupid', 'I am not normal');
- Research that involves the collection of human tissue, blood or other biological samples.

With this in mind it is important that psychologists consider the guidelines and code of ethics set out by the BPS very carefully and pay particular attention to the following issues.

- **Is the research based on theories that may contain any biases, controversies or ethical issues**
- **The implications of investigating certain topics**
- **How the research findings will be used**
- **Their position in society and their influence on public policy**
- **How the findings will be reported and distributed**

It is important to note that socially sensitive research may not just affect the participants, it can produce a risk or threat to their family or friends, the researcher and other members of the research team. According to McCosker et al. (2001) it is important that adequate safeguards are built into the research, through appropriate training and access to counselling when necessary.

For more information about The Code of Human Research Ethics (2014) click here or visit http://www.bps.org.uk/system/files/Public%20files/code_of_human_research_ethics_dec_201 4_inf180_web.pdf

In the table below, give an example of how the research studies or theories are examples of socially sensitive research.

Study/Research	Eye Witness Testimony	Rushton's IQ Tests	Bowlby's Maternal Deprivation	Social Influence Research
Ethical issues or bias with the research or theory				Deception
How the findings were used	Shaped police interview techniques			
Social status of researcher		Highly regarded university professor that published numerous books and articles		
Implications				Outlined that anyone can be influenced by authority – even if this goes against their morals
How the findings were reported			World Health Organization recommendation that children need their mother's care to develop normally	

Debates in Psychology

Learning Objectives

On completion of this unit you should be familiar with the following:

- Free will and determinism
- Idiographic and nomothetic approaches
- The nature-nurture debate
- Holism and reductionism

This unit looks at some of the main philosophical debates in psychology in detail. You have been introduced to the issues in the previous section and like the issues, debates in psychology run throughout the course. In the exam you will be expected to demonstrate your knowledge and understanding of how they have shaped research and topics in psychology.

All the research, theories and approaches that you look at in psychology have their strengths and limitations and the ability to evaluate these effectively is crucial in the development of your knowledge and understanding of human behaviour.

To get you thinking about the different issues and debates in psychology – complete the table below using your previous knowledge of the approaches and choose their position on the following debates.

Approaches	Free will or Determinism?	Reductionist or Holistic?	Nature or Nurture?	Idiographic or Nomothetic?
Learning Approaches	*Determinism*			
Cognitive Approach		*Reductionist*		
Biological Approach			*Nature*	
Psychodynamic Approach			*Both*	
Humanistic Psychology				*Idiographic*

In the table below, give an example of a theory, research or concept that illustrates the position of each approach in relation to the debate.

Approaches	Free will or Determinism?	Reductionist or Holistic?	Nature or Nurture?	Idiographic or Nomothetic?
Learning Approaches	Aggression is learnt through imitation = Determinism			
Cognitive Approach		Multi-store Model of Memory = Reductionist		
Biological Approach			All behaviour is determined by our genetics = nature	
Psychodynamic Approach				Little Hans case study = idiographic
Humanistic Psychology	Claims that all individuals can choose their own actions = Free will			

1. Free will and determinism: hard determinism and soft determinism

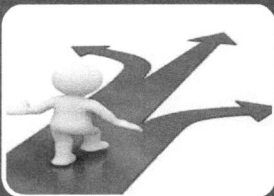

Free Will
- The concept that individuals make their own decisions and have the ability to choose their behaviour and the direction that their life will take

Determinism
- The concept that all behaviour is caused by either internal (e.g.genetics) or external factors (e.g. social learning) or past experiences

Hard determinism believes that all behaviour is linked to something outside a person's control. But there are serious implications with this idea as it implies that we cannot be punished for our behaviour as we cannot be held accountable for our actions.

The idea of free-will is also problematic, as many would argue that there is no such thing as free-will. Psychologists address this through the notion of soft-determinism, William James (1890) suggested that behaviour is determined by a person's own character traits, goals and conscious beliefs. As long as our actions are voluntary and we are doing what is best for us then it is regarded as being free-will. So, if behaviour is controlled by these factors there is causation but it is free from coercion (force) or constraint.

The psychological approaches we have looked at previously all adopt a position on the free will and determinism debate depending on their main assumptions about human behaviour.

Briefly explain why behaviourism is considered to be a deterministic approach.

....

....

....

....

(2 marks)

Outline how the humanistic approach supports the free will debate in psychology.

....

....

....

....

....

(2 marks)

The biological approach claims that mental disorders are caused by chemical imbalances, therefore is deterministic. True or False?

True ☐   False ☐

(1 mark)

Which of the following statements (A – D) about the free will v determinism debate are true. Circle the two correct answers.

A   The psychodynamic approach's belief that all behaviour is linked to childhood conflicts is deterministic

B   The biological approach assumes that we are free to choose our own behaviour

C   The cognitive approach claim that schemas influence behaviour is deterministic

D   The behavioural approach supports free will

(2 marks)

Different types of determinism

As you have already noticed most of the psychological approaches reject the notion of free will and support the determinism argument. This is mainly due to the fact that they have a scientific emphasis on causal explanations of behaviour i.e. manipulation of the IV will determine the outcome on the DV, so cause and effect is established. On the other hand, the concept of free-will and soft-determinism and the behaviours that are affected cannot be tested using scientific methods.

From the approaches a variety of different types of determinism have emerged.

Biological Determinism — **Biological Approach**

- Behaviour is controlled by internal factors within our biology e.g. genes and chemicals
- Implies that all behaviour or mental disorders are inherited

Environmental Determinism — **Learning Approaches**

- Behaviour is controlled by external factors and influences e.g. parents and society
- Implies that all behaviour is learned by social interaction

Psychic Determinism — **Psychodynamic Approach**

- All behaviour is controlled by unconscious fears and/or desires
- Implies that all behaviour is linked to previous childhood events or experiences

Biological determinism implies that behaviour is controlled by genetic factors. True or False?

True ☐   False ☐

(1 mark)

People from depression often say that the condition runs in their family. However, DSM-5 highlights that many depressed people have serious social problems and therapists have reported that many of their patients have experienced traumatic experiences in early childhood.

With reference to the scenario above, explain what is meant by determinism. Refer to three types of determinism in your answer.

....

....

....

....

....

....

....

....

....

....

....

....

....

(6 marks)

Outline the difference between soft determinism and hard determinism.

....

....

....

....

(2 marks)

2. Idiographic and nomothetic approaches to psychological investigation

The approaches in psychology take either an idiographic or nomothetic approach when studying human behaviour.

Idiographic

- Humans are unique and should be studied in an individual way to capture richness and detail
- It makes use of non-experimental methods such as case studies and autobiographies
- The approach is concerned with qualitative data
- Is an effective approach when dealing with highly sensitive issues
- Can provide a starting point for further research
- Difficult to generalise any findings to the wider population
- Research methods are subjective and open to researcher bias

Nomothetic

- Involves studying large samples to create general laws that can apply to all
- It uses scientific methods such as experiments
- The approach is concerned with quantitative data
- The emphasis on behaviour that can be measured and controlled objectively makes is scientifically reliable and valid
- It does not take into account individual differences in behaviour i.e. two people may be diagnosed with the same mental disorder but they may no necessarily display the same symptoms
- Although it predicts group behaviour it does not fully explain or predict an individual's behaviour

Which approach is adopted when carrying out psychological investigations usually depends on what is being studied and what the purpose of the research is. So, if a researcher is interested in looking at aggressive behaviour in terms of its general features then a nomothetic approach would be adopted, with the researcher using a large sample of the general population, using a testable hypothesis and analysing the data using quantitative methods.

However, if a researcher wanted to look at and predict the aggressive behaviour of a particular individual, then an idiographic approach would be preferable, using individual interviews to record their childhood experiences and thoughts about their aggression or asking the individual to keep a diary to gather rich and detailed qualitative data.

In reality, many psychological investigations use a combination of both approaches with individual cases providing a starting point or catalyst for more extensive research that can be used to support or challenge accepted theories.

Outline the difference between an idiographic and a nomothetic approach.

....

....

....

....

....

(2 marks)

An educational psychologist used an idiographic approach to study exam stress. She asked two students to write down their thoughts about the amount of pressure they felt from others and how this made them feel about their exams over a period of two months. Qualitative analysis of their diaries showed that the students felt under pressure from parents and teachers and that this had a negative effect on exam revision.

Explain how a researcher would carry out the above investigation using a nomothetic approach.

....

....

....

....

....

....

....

....

....

....

....

....

....

(6 marks)

3. The nature-nurture debate

The nature-nurture debate is a philosophical argument between those psychologists who believe that behaviour is influenced by innate biological factors, known as nativism and those who believe that behaviour is a result of external environmental factors, known as empiricism.

The main characteristics of both arguments are outlined below.

Nature

- Nativist philosophy
- Biology & Genetics
- Behaviour caused by genetics, inherited traits, chemical imbalances
- Scientific method used e.g. scans, drug therapy, twin & family studies
- Behaviour can only be changed through physical means
- Reductionist as it ignores the role of environmental factors

Nurture

- Emipiricist philosophy
- Social learning
- Behaviour is learnt through experiences with the environment
- Scientific methods used to manipulate external factors to study behaviour
- Behaviour can only be modified through changing environmental conditions
- Reductionist as it ignores the role of biological factors

Explain how the nature debate in psychology is biologically deterministic.

....

....

....

....

(2 marks)

Explain how the nurture debate in psychology is environmentally deterministic.

....

....

....

....

(2 marks)

Heredity and Environment

So as we have already mentioned the nature-nurture debate centres around the role of heredity (inherited factors) and the environment in influencing behaviour. Today, psychologists are not concerned with taking one side or the other, instead they tend to focus their research on investigating which side of the argument has the most influence over our behaviour. This is done through the use of twin and family studies.

Twin studies are investigations carried out on identical monozygotic (MZ) or non-identical dizygotic (DZ) twins who have been raised together or apart. These studies are designed to assess the relative importance of heredity and environment in behaviour and they produce **heritability coefficients estimates**, which tell us how strong the relationship is between our behaviour and our heredity.

Key Term

Heritability coefficients estimates
A statistical estimate of the proportion of the difference in some behaviour or trait that is due to genetic differences among individuals in the population.

Concordance Rate
The degree to which similar traits are shared

Research into the nature side of the debate carried out by Carey and Gottesman (1981) found an 87% **concordance rate** in MZ twins suffering from OCD and a 47% concordance in DZ twins. Therefore, they concluded that they must have had a genetic predisposition for developing OCD. Similar findings were recorded by McKeon and Murray (1987), who found that patients with OCD were more likely to have first degree relatives who suffered from an anxiety disorder. Additionally, research into the IQ of MZ and DZ twins carried out by Bouchard and McGue (1981) found that the concordance rate of the MZ twins was higher than the DZ twins, showing a clear genetic influence.

Genetic studies do not produce a 100% concordance rate, of both twins having the same behaviour or trait, so there must be environmental influences too. Behaviourist psychologists argue that behaviour develops as a result of operant or classical conditioning and social learning as outlined in the research carried out by Bandura.

Outline what is meant by the nature-nurture debate in psychology.

....

....

....

....

....

(2 marks)

The Interactionist Approach

Many of the traditional studies that looked at the nature-nurture debate have taken a dichotomous view of human behaviour, that is they have looked at the issue from a completely separate viewpoint. The interactionist approach in psychology claims that nature and nature do not work independently of one another, they interact with another.

According to Plomin et al (1977) interaction between heredity and environment can occur in three different ways:

Passive heredity - environmental interaction
Sporty parents may provide an environment that is very sporty for their children. The environment is linked to the parent's genetic make-up and passively transmitted to their children via their home environment

Reactive heredity - environmental interaction
A parent may react more positively to a child who is easy going and happy than a moody and demanding child. The home environment is a reaction to the genetic predisposition of the child

Active heredity - environmental interaction
A sociable child is more likely to seek out friends who are similar and engage with different people, than a shy child. The genetic make-up of the child seeks to develop in an environment that is similar to their predisposed characteristics

As a result, it is generally accepted that the interaction between heredity and environment form a continuum, in which it is difficult to separate the two factors when looking at human behaviour.

The approaches in psychology sit on a continuum as follows. In the table below each approach summarise its position in relation to the nature-nurture debate.

Nature				Nurture
Biopsychology	Psychodynamic	Cognitive	Humanistic	Behaviourist

(6 marks)

The nature debate in psychology claims that behaviour is influenced by innate biological factors. True or False?

True ☐ False ☐

(1 mark)

Concordance rate refers to the degree to which similar traits are shared. True or False?

True ☐ False ☐

(1 mark)

Discuss the nature-nurture debate in psychology. Refer to at least two topics you have studied in your answer.

....

....

....

....

....

....

....

....

....

....

....

....

....

....

....

....

....

....

....

....

....

....

....

....

....

....

....

....

....

....

....

....

....

....

....

....

....

....

....

....

....

....

....

....

....

....

....

....

....

....

....

....

....

....

....

....

....

....

....

....

....

....

....

....

....

....

(16 marks)

4. Holism and reductionism: levels of explanation in Psychology

The holism-reductionism debate in psychology is the argument between psychologists about the best way to study complex human behaviour. Reductionism works on the scientific assumption of parsimony, that is the principle of explaining a phenomenon in terms of its constituent parts. The earliest examples of this are found in structuralism, where Wundt's explains conscious experience in terms of images, feelings and sensation i.e. its constituent parts.

In order to achieve a reductionist explanation, a psychologist will use a hierarchy of explanation to study the underlying causes of the behaviour, explained in the pyramid below.

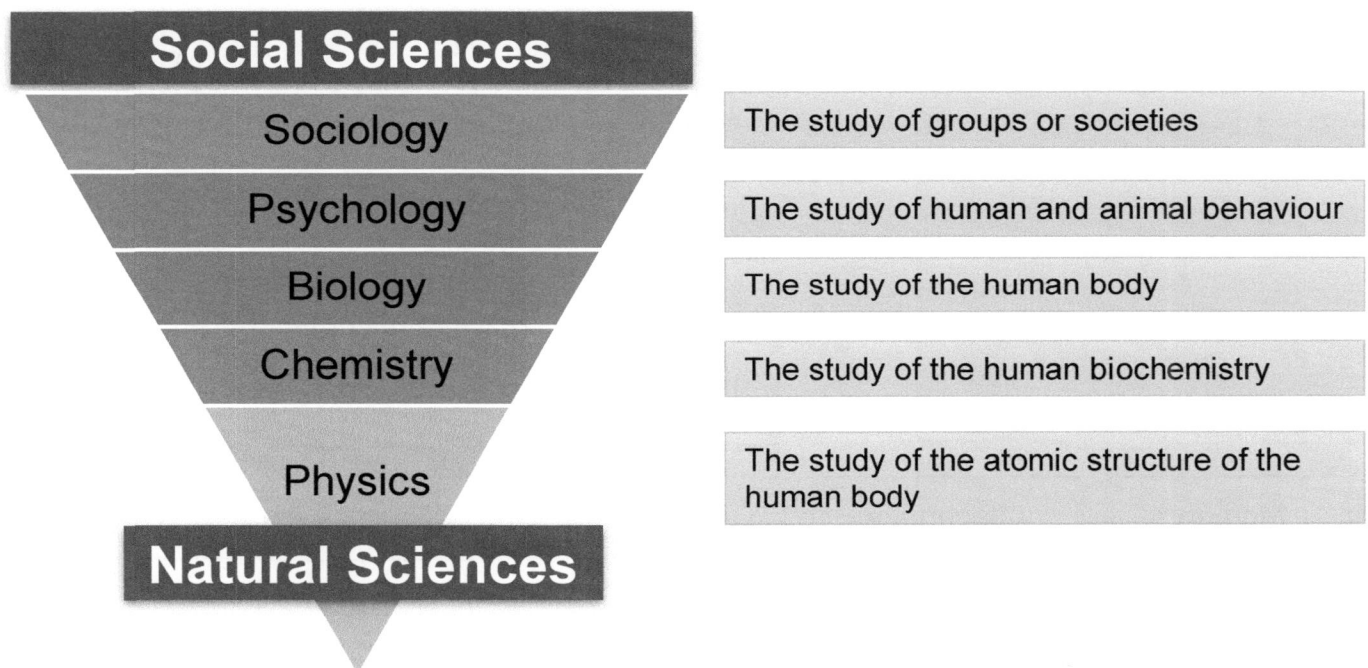

Social Sciences	
Sociology	The study of groups or societies
Psychology	The study of human and animal behaviour
Biology	The study of the human body
Chemistry	The study of the human biochemistry
Physics	The study of the atomic structure of the human body
Natural Sciences	

So, as you can see from the pyramid, a behaviour is first observed within a group at the higher social science level and then studied at a more individual level within psychology. It can then be broken down further into the physiological explanations of the natural sciences lower down in the hierarchical levels of explanation.

To show that you fully understand the term reductionism, you will need to be able to explain how the research or theory is being reductionist and outline whether this is good or bad. The two main types of reductionism you will come across are:

- Environmental Reductionism – explaining behaviour in terms of the higher level explanations; environmental factors and stimulus response experiences (S-R) i.e. classical and operant conditioning
- Biological Reductionism – explaining behaviour in terms of the lower levels of explanation; the physical causes such as genetics, biochemistry and neuroanatomy

Critics argue that the cognitive approach is an example of machine reductionism. Explain why this might be the case.

....

....

....

....

(2 marks)

Critics argue that the psychodynamic approach is an example of psychic reductionism. Explain why this might be the case.

....

....

....

....

(2 marks)

From each topic in the table below, give an example of a theory or research that is limited by reductionism.

Memory	Attachment	Depression	Phobias	OCD

(6 marks)

Evaluation of Reductionism

Strengths

- Parsimony makes it economical and easy to study complex human behaviour. For example, behavioural studies that only focus on simple S-R responses are parsimonious unlike psychodynamic theories that look at a variety of explanations.
- Reductionism is used in the natural sciences and is viewed by the scientific community as being highly scientific and analytic. Therefore, it has greater support and credibility leading to a more concrete understanding.
- Reducing phenomena to its constituent parts enables psychologists to clearly operationalise and control variables and make predictions about the outcome of scientific investigations and replication is possible.
- Reductionism enables psychologists to look at complex mental disorders, identify the cause and provide effective treatment. For example, in psychopathology, biopsychologists study MZ twins to determine the concordance rate of one twin developing schizophrenia if the other has the disorder in order to develop effective gene therapy treatments.

Weaknesses

- Oversimplifying complex human behaviour can ignore the richness of behaviour at the higher levels of explanations i.e. it does not look at the context in which behaviour emerges so that value of reducing behaviour to its constituent parts may be limited
- Reductionism may lead to a lack of validity as it may not be measuring what it claims to be measuring. For example, a biochemical reaction does not tell us what emotion is felt, that will rely on the higher conscious psychology level of explanation where the patient tells the researcher how they are feeling

Reductionism in psychology is the principle of explaining a phenomenon in terms of its constituent parts. True or False?

True ☐   False ☐

(1 mark)

Reducing phenomena to its constituent parts makes it difficult to investigate behaviour using scientific methods. True or False?

True ☐   False ☐

(1 mark)

The idea that human behaviour can be explained by looking at constituent parts is a very narrow view. Holism on the other hand, argues that in order to fully understand human behaviour psychologists need to take the view "that the whole is greater than the sum of its parts". This can involve looking at the whole individual, the whole system, the whole behaviour, the whole experience or an interaction between all of these levels.

Examples of holism can be found in the following:

Gestalt Psychology

- Explains behaviour by looking at the individual as a whole
- Used mainly when looking at perception
- Kohler (1925) found that chimpanzees, after attempting to reach a banana using its arm unsuccessfully, then spontaneaously picked up a stick to help it without any prior S-R learning. He called this insight learning

Humanistic Psychology

- Investigates the individual as a whole - body and mind
- According to Rogers and Maslow the concept of self-actualisation is a basic drive that when fulfilled gives purpose and motivation to the whole individual

Interactionist Approach

- Claims that the different levels of explanation interact with one another and that all factors should be taken into account when explaining human behaviour
- Freud's psychodynamic approach emphasises the dynamic interaction between the id, ego and superego
- Mental illness is usually explained by a combination of biological, social and psychological factors

Social Psychology

- Explains individual behaviour within a social context and argues that group behaviour shows characteristics that are greater than the sum of the individual parts
- Examples are found in the social influence topic; deindividuation and Zimabrdo's research

Outline what is meant by the holism-reductionism debate in psychology.

....

....

....

....

....

(2 marks)

Holism is the idea that in order to fully understand human behaviour psychologists need to study the individual as a whole. True or False?

True ☐   False ☐

(1 mark)

Evaluation of Holism

Strengths

- Holistic explanations of behaviour can integrate many different levels of explanations and provide a more complete picture than reductionist approaches
- These explanations provide an eclectic approach to therapy, using both drugs and psychotherapy to effectively treat serious mental disorders
- Holism is a more functional explanation, providing reasons why people behave in a certain way e.g. aggression, rather than just focusing on the biological cause of behaviour. It can therefore be used more effectively in talking therapies.
- Higher level explanations of behaviour are not scared to investigate the complexity of human behaviour and acknowledge the importance of social interaction in creating new behaviour. This would be ignored by the lower levels of explanation.

Weaknesses

- Holistic explanations are less scientific than reductionist explanations
- Holistic investigations are less economical and more difficult to control
- Holism tends to ignore the huge influence of biology on behaviour
- The explanations within holism tend to be more hypothetical the higher up the levels of explanation, leading to a lack of predictive power compared to the natural sciences at the lower levels of explanation

Discuss the holism-reductionism debate in psychology. Refer to at least two topics you have studied in your answer.

....

....

....

....

....

....

....

....

....

....

....

....

....

....

....

....

....

....

....

....

....

....

....

....

....

....

....

....

....

....

....

....

....

....

....

....

....

....

....

....

....

....

....

....

....

....

....

....

....

....

....

....

....

....

....

....

....

....

....

....

....

....

....

....

....

....

....

(16 marks)

Cognition and Development

Learning Objectives

On completion of this unit you should be familiar with the following:

- Piaget's theory of cognitive development: schemas, assimilation, accommodation, equilibration, stages of intellectual development. Characteristics of these stages, including object permanence, conservation, egocentrism and class inclusion.
- Vygotsky's theory of cognitive development, including the zone of proximal development and scaffolding.
- Baillargeon's explanation of early infant abilities, including knowledge of the physical world; violation of expectation research.
- The development of social cognition: Selman's levels of perspective-taking; theory of mind, including theory of mind as an explanation for autism; the Sally-Anne study. The role of the mirror neuron system in social cognition.

Cognition is a complex process that involves both biological and psychological factors. In this unit we will look at how young children develop cognitive skills such as problem solving, perspective taking and empathy that enable them to form meaningful social relationships.

Piaget

Learning Objectives

On completion of this section you should be familiar with:

1. Piaget's theory of cognitive development: schemas, assimilation, accommodation, equilibration
2. Stages of intellectual development
3. Characteristics of these stages, including object permanence, conservation, egocentrism and class inclusion

During the 1950's and 60's research into cognitive development began focusing on our inner thought processes and how these change over the course of our life in an attempt to explain the different behaviour shown at different ages. Many psychologists have attempted to explain what causes these cognitive changes, focusing on the role of genetics and the influence of the environment. The most notable cognitive developmental researchers are Piaget and Vygotsky and this unit will outline and evaluate their theories and examine how they have shaped our understanding of cognitive development.

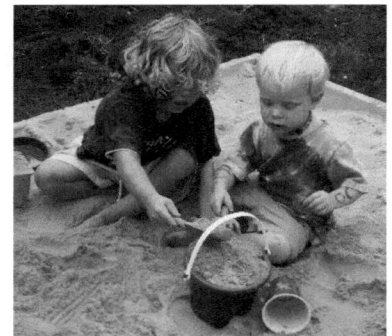

The cognitive approach is one of the most dominant approaches in psychology as it uses highly scientific methods to investigate internal mental processes. Outline one advantage of this methodology when studying human behaviour.

....

....

....

....

(2 marks)

The cognitive approach in psychology assumes that our internal mental processes are influenced by schemas. Outline what is meant by the term schema.

....

....

....

....

(2 marks)

1. Piaget's theory of cognitive development

One of the first researchers and most well known in the field of cognitive development is Jean Piaget (1896 – 1980), who believed that intelligence was not a fixed trait but a complex interaction between biological maturation (nature) and adaptation to the demands of the environment (nurture). Piaget claimed that children learn through active interaction with the world around them and that this intellectual development occurs in stages.

Schemas

One of the key concepts in Piaget's theory of cognitive development is the role of schema, which he defined as "a cohesive, repeatable action sequence possessing component actions that are tightly interconnected and governed by a core meaning". Put simply, Piaget believed that a schema is an innate building block, which helps an infant to make sense of the world around them and become more intelligent. For example, a baby is born with certain innate reflex schema, such as sucking or gripping and they use these to explore the world around them. As the infant grows older, the amount of schemas increases and they become more complex as they continue to construct their understanding of the world. Piaget, claimed that once these schemas have developed, these mental representations are stored and then used to understand and respond to situations when needed. According to Wadsworth (2004) schemas are like 'index cards' filed in the brain, each one telling an individual how to react to incoming stimuli or information.

According to Piaget's theory of cognitive development infants are born with innate schemas. Briefly outline the role of schemas in cognitive development.

....

....

....

....

....

....

....

....

(4 marks)

Assimilation, Accommodation and Equilibration

According to Piaget, children construct their understanding about the world around them through the following processes:

<table>
<tr>
<td>Assimilation</td>
<td>
• Existing schemas are used to make sense of and understand new situations, objects or ideas
• The world outside is adapted to fit in to what the child already knows
</td>
</tr>
<tr>
<td>Accommodation</td>
<td>
• Exisiting schemas fail to deal with new situations, objects or ideas
• New schemas are formed or existing schemas are expanded
</td>
</tr>
<tr>
<td>Equilibration</td>
<td>
• An individual strives to keep an internal state of equilibrium (balance)
• All new new situations, objects or ideas will lead to disequilibrium, which causes imbalance (stress)
• Returning to the assimilation and accommodation stages to make sense of the new information
</td>
</tr>
</table>

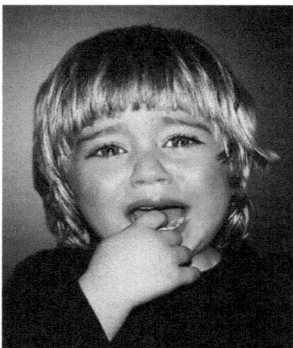

So, a child will actively explore and discover its environment using their existing schemas to make sense of what they find (assimilation). If everything makes sense the child is happy and is said to be in a state of equilibrium (balance). However, if the child encounters something new that cannot be accommodated by an existing schema, the child becomes distressed. This is said to be a state of disequilibrium and the child seeks ways to return to a state of balance as quickly as possible. In an attempt to do this, existing schemas are modified to deal with the new situation, leading to the formation of new or more complex schemas (accommodation). This process is the fundamental basis of Piaget's theory of cognitive development.

A stressful state of disequilibrium occurs when new information cannot be fitted into existing schemas. True or false?

True ☐ False ☐

(1 mark)

Explain what is meant by the term assimilation in Piaget's theory of cognitive development.

....

....

....

....

....

....

(2 marks)

Explain what is meant by the term accommodation in Piaget's theory of cognitive development.

....

....

....

....

....

....

(2 marks)

Explain what is meant by the term equilibration in Piaget's theory of cognitive development.

....

....

....

....

....

....

(2 marks)

A mother takes her child to the swimming pool and takes their armbands off for the first time. The child cries and refuses to get into the water, so the mother encourages the child by guiding them in the water and after a short time the child stops crying and begins splashing on their own.

Using Piaget's theory of cognitive development explain the process the child in this scenario has experienced.

....

....

....

....

....

....

....

....

....

....

....

....

....

....

....

....

....

....

....

....

(6 marks)

2. Stages of intellectual development

Piaget proposed that infants go through four universal stages of intellectual development. He claimed that each stage is determined by the innate biological changes that occur in every child and so will reflect the increasing sophistication of a child's thought processes. In addition, Piaget believed that although the age at which the child will reach each stage may differ, the sequence of the stages is the same for all children.

The four stages of intellectual development are outlined below.

Sensorimotor - birth to 2 years old

- An infant's thought process can be measured by observing simple reflex actions and whether they can differentiate themselves from objects

Pre-operational - 2 to 7 years old

- This stage is characterised by the ability to learn language and to be able to use it to describe objects and images, but reasoning is limited

Concrete Operations - 7 to 12 years old

- A child's intelligence can be measured by their ability to think logically about objects and events

Formal Operations - 12 years onwards

- A child will approach problems in a systematic way and have the ability to think about abstract concepts and make logical hypothetical deductions about problems

Outline the two assumptions of Piaget's stage theory of intellectual development.

....

....

....

....

....

(2 marks)

According to Piaget, children in the pre-operational stage have limited logical reasoning abilities. True or false?

True ☐   False ☐

(1 mark)

Briefly outline the four stages of Piaget's theory of intellectual development.

....

....

....

....

....

....

....

....

....

....

....

....

(4 marks)

3. Characteristics of these stages

Research in support of Piaget's stages of cognitive development is drawn from his many years of observing infants and children. Using the clinical method, Piaget got to know the individual children before asking them a series of questions in an unstandardised way. For example, different materials would be presented to different children according to their individual characteristics.

Outline one limitation with the clinical method used by Piaget to study the stages of intellectual development.

....

....

....

....

....

(2 marks)

We will now take a closer look at each of the stages, with specific reference to the concepts of object permanence, conservation, egocentrism and class inclusion and evaluate the contribution Piaget has made to our understanding of how intelligence develops.

Sensorimotor Stage (0 – 2 years)

In the early part of the sensorimotor stage, Piaget claimed that an infant's schemas consist only of their innate reflex actions, such as sucking or gripping. According to Piaget this is demonstrated by:

- **Egocentrism** – the infant is unable to distinguish between itself and the environment around them
- **Object Permanence** – if the infant cannot see or touch an object it ceases to exist for them

Piaget investigated object permanence by hiding objects under a cover. He found that young infants up to five months of age showed no signs of searching for the hidden objects that they had previously been interested in, but by eight months old the same children searched for the object even when hidden. Bower and Wishart (1972) disputed Piaget's findings and demonstrated that a child aged between one and four months continued to search for an object even when the lights were switched off in their controlled observations. Further research by Bower (1977) found that infants as young as one month old showed surprise that a toy placed behind a screen was not present when the screen was removed, this demonstrated that the infant had an understanding of object permanence.

Outline what is meant by the term egocentrism in Piaget's sensorimotor stage of intellectual development.

....

....

....

....

(1 marks)

Outline what is meant by the term object permanence in Piaget's sensorimotor stage of intellectual development.

....

....

....

....

(1 marks)

Pre-operational Stage (2 - 7 years)

During this stage the infant's intellectual development continues as their internal mental schemas become more complex. Piaget believed that the use of symbolic representations such as language in the pre-operational stage is a sign of rapid and fundamental cognitive development. However, much of their behaviour is characterised by:

- **Egocentrism** – children assume everyone else thinks or sees things in the same way as they do
- **Class-inclusion** – they have not developed an understanding that an object may be a sub-set of a larger class and so only focus on the most obvious class. For example, there is a class of objects known as cats and also a class known as animals. A cat is an animal and is therefore also a sub-set of the larger animal class.
- **Conservation** – at this stage the children display a lack of conservation as they do not have the ability to realise that although the visible appearance of an object may change it actually remains constant

According to Piaget, the characteristics of the pre-operational stage show that children are only able to see the world from their own perspective and as a consequence are only able to focus on one object or situation at a time, a term he called centration. In his class-inclusion tasks, Piaget children were shown a set of beads, most of which were brown with a few white beads and then asked "are there more brown beads, or more beads?" Most of the children answered that there were more brown beads. Piaget argued that this demonstrated that children did not understand the concept class inclusion, that is that all the members of one sub-set (the brown beads) can belong to another, larger class (the beads).

Outline what is meant by the term class-inclusion in Piaget's pre-operational stage of intellectual development.

....

....

....

....

(1 mark)

However, research carried out by McGarrigle et al (1978) looked at whether the language used affected the way the children answered the questions regarding class-inclusion. In the study, 35 six year-olds were shown three toy black cows and one toy white cow. The cows were then placed on their sides and the children were told that the cows were sleeping. The researchers then asked the children two questions:

1. 'Are there more black cows or more cows'
2. 'Are there more black cows or more sleeping cows'

They found that 25% of the children answered question one correctly compared to 48% for question two. Suggesting that children in the pre-operational stage have the ability to recognise class-inclusion when questions are asked in a way that is appropriate for their age.

There are methodological issues with the questions Piaget asked the children when investigating class-inclusion. Identify one methodological issue and explain what effect it might have had on the findings of Piaget's research.

....

....

....

....

....

....

....

....

(3 marks)

To demonstrate the influence centration has on the characteristic of egocentrism, Piaget and Inhelder (1956) carried out their famous 'Three Mountains Experiment'. The aim of their study was to determine the children's ability to take the visual perspective of another person. One hundred children aged between 4 and 12 years old were shown a model of three mountains and given three shaped and coloured cards, which matched the mountains. The children were then asked to arrange the cards to show what could be seen by someone looking at the model from a different position. In addition the children were asked to select the picture that best showed the view seen by a doll when it was placed at different positions in relation to the mountains. Piaget and Inhelder found that children under 8 years old were unable to distinguish between the scene they were looking at and the viewpoint as seen by someone else, while those over the age of nine were more successful. So, supporting Piaget's stage theory of intellectual development.

Piaget and Inhelder's (1956) 'Three Mountains Experiment' is often criticised as it lacks mundane realism. Outline what is meant by the term mundane realism in relation to this experiment.

....

....

....

....

....

....

(2 mark)

Piaget and Inhelder's (1956) 'Three Mountain Experiment' asked young children to make sense of a very complicated image. Outline what effect this might have had on the findings of this research study.

....

....

....

....

....

....

(2 mark)

To investigate the criticisms that Piaget and Inhelder's (1956) 'Three Mountains Experiment' was not an appropriate test of egocentrism, Hughes and Donaldson (1978) carried out a study to investigate children's ability to take another person's point of view. Using a model of two intersecting walls and a doll of a little boy and two policeman dolls, 30 children aged between 3 and 5 years old were asked to hide the doll so that the policemen could not see it in many different configurations. They found that pre-school children selected a correct hiding place for the doll 90% of the time. Hughes and Donaldson argued that their simpler methods, which resembled a game of hide-and-seek, were more age appropriate and showed that Piaget's stage theory underestimated children's intellectual development.

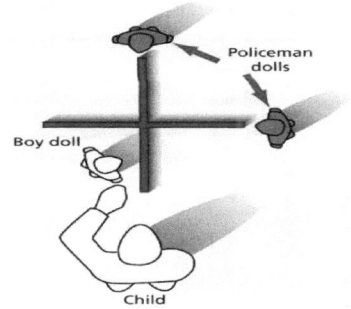

Piaget also carried out many experiments that tested the characteristic of conservation in the in children and found that at this stage, they were unable to recognise that when nothing is added or taken away from and object or substance, the amount remains the same regardless of changes in shape or appearance. Piaget believed that centration prevented children at this stage being able to conserve.

Explain what is meant by the term conservation in Piaget's Stage Theory of intellectual development.

....

....

....

....

(2 mark)

Outline what is meant by the term centration in Piaget's Stage Theory of intellectual development.

....

....

....

....

(2 mark)

According to Piaget, children in the pre-operational stage are unable to take the visual perspective of another person. True or false?

True ☐   False ☐

(1 mark)

Piaget conducted many studies looking at how conservation is affected by a child's centration, and one of the most famous is the conservation of liquid tasks carried out during the 1960's.

Aim

Piaget was interested in looking at how centration prevents children in the pre-operational stage understanding conservation

Procedure

- Children under 7 years of age were presented with two identical glasses containing equal amounts of liquid
- The children were asked to confirm that they understand that they both contain the same amount of liquid
- The juice from one glass was then poured into a tall, thin glass
- The child was then asked if the tall glass and original glass contain the same amount of liquid

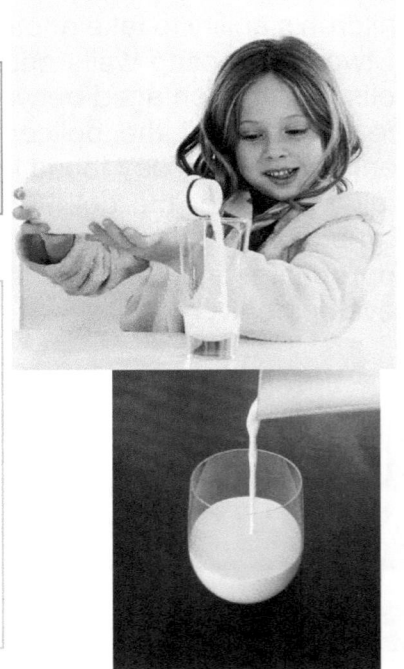

Results

- Children reported that there was more liquid in the tall, thin glass because the juice is taller or it is higher

Conclusions

- Piaget concluded that this demonstrated that children in the pre-operational stage could only focus on one aspect at a time. So, when the liquid is poured into the tall glass they do not notice that the width of the original glass makes up for the height of the new container.

Piaget also argued that along with centration, the child at this stage of development also lacks important cognitive operations, which he called reversibility and syncretic thought. According to Piaget, the children cannot recognise that the procedure can be repeated in the opposite direction (reversed) as they lack the cognitive schema that enables them to mentally reverse an action. In addition, they are unable to take into account more than one aspect of a situation at any one time, therefore lack syncretic thought.

According to Piaget, children in the pre-operational stage have the ability to take account of more than one aspect of a situation at the same time. True or false?

True ☐ False ☐

(1 mark)

Briefly explain what Piaget's conservation tasks tell us about the intellectual development of children in the pre-operational stage.

....

....

....

....

....

....

....

....

....

....

....

....

(4 marks)

Research carried out by Rose and Blank (1974) and Samuel and Bryant (1984) suggests that the children in Piaget's conservation tasks may have been confused by the questions asked, i.e. they were asked two questions by the experimenter, so they may have thought that they were expecting two different answers. They found that when the children were only asked to make one judgment, they responded better to the task. However, although an increased number of younger children did answer correctly when only asked one question it was still noted that older children were better able to cope with the task.

Outline two factors, other than those outlined by Piaget's observations, that may have had an effect on the children's responses in the conservation tasks.

....

....

....

....

....

(2 marks)

Concrete Operations Stage (7 – 11 years)

In this third stage, Piaget argued that children no longer display egocentrism or centration and can carry out complex cognitive operations, that involve conservation and reversibility. After conducting many observations and experiments on conservation, Piaget claimed that a child in concrete operational stage can recognise that numbers, mass and weights remain constant despite the alteration in appearance. When the same amount of liquid (a) is poured into a taller/thinner beaker (b) a concrete operational child will recognise that the amount of liquid in both beakers (c) remain the same. In addition, at this stage they begin to mentally reverse the act of pouring, which enables them to recognise that the amount of liquid remains the same. According to Piaget, this higher-level of intellectual development, where the child is able to look beyond immediate appearance and focus on more than one aspect of a situation at the same time, occurs at 8 years of age. However, Piaget concluded that at this stage of development children were better at 'concrete' tasks rather than abstract tasks.

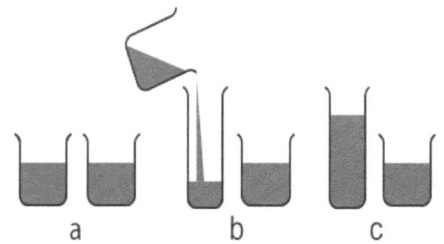

Formal Operations Stage (12 years onwards)

In Piaget's final formal operational stage of cognitive development, the child masters the ability to carry out logical reasoning, without the need for concrete examples. Piaget carried out a series of deductive reasoning tasks, such as "if A > B > C, then A > C" and found that in all cases the child could solve the problems. In addition, at this stage of development children are able to carry out tasks in a logical and systematic way, demonstrated in the pendulum swing test in which the children were able to work out how the different weights affected the swing of the pendulum.

Many of Piaget's experiments have been criticised as they fail to take into account the child's understanding and as a result may have led the child to give socially desirable answers.

Outline what is meant by the term socially desirable and explain how it might have affected the findings of Piaget's experiments and observations.

....

....

....

....

....

....

....

....

(4 marks)

It is often said that Piaget's stage theory of intellectual development ignores the social process involved in cognitive development. Explain why this is an issue when explaining human behaviour.

....

....

....

....

....

(2 marks)

Piaget assumed that maturation of the brain plays an important role in allowing children to progress through the stages of cognitive development. True or false?

True ☐   False ☐

(1 mark)

Evaluation

Strengths

- Piaget was the first person to investigate and attempt to explain how children's thinking changes as they develop
- His work has been very influential and has sparked huge interest in this field, widening our understanding of cognitive development
- Many educational practices and teaching methods have been developed as a direct result of Piaget's work and take into account the different stages of intellectual development

Limitations

- Piaget's theory is more descriptive than explanatory
- Some of the stages appear to overlap, so it may be better to describe cognitive development as a continuous process rather than a four stage process
- Piaget claimed that children who failed to complete a task lacked the necessary cognitive functions and ignored other factors that might have explained the failure such as the children simply didn't understand the task
- By focusing on the things that children lack, Piaget failed to recognise the important abilities that children possess at various stages of their development
- Piaget's theory does not account for other cognitive factors that could explain the individual differences in development found, such as memory, practice or motivation.

Outline three limitations of using Piaget's research to explain cognitive development.

....

....

....

....

....

....

....

....

....

....

....

....

....

....

....

....

....

....

....

....

....

....

....

(6 marks)

Vygotsky

Learning Objectives

On completion of this section you should be familiar with:

1. Vygotsky's theory of cognitive development, including the zone of proximal development and scaffolding.

As we have seen, Piaget's theory has been criticised by some researchers as it neglects the role of social influences and overemphasises the role of maturation in cognitive development. We will now look at research carried out by the Russian psychologist Lev Vygotsky, that has attempted to address these criticisms in an attempt to develop a more holistic theory of cognitive development.

1. Vygotsky's theory of cognitive development

Vygotsky (1896-1934) believed that social learning precedes cognitive development and that social interaction provides the meaning for the child to make sense of their environment. Vygotsky claimed that cognitive development first occurs on a social and cultural level as the child interacts with others (interpsychological). Later the child internalises what they have learnt (intrapsychological) and then uses these skills to enhance their cognitive development. The greatest development comes when the infant begins to grasp and internalise language, Vygotsky believed that this was essential as a tool for communicating social rules and providing guidance in problem solving.

Both Piaget and Vygotsky noted that pre-school children will talk to themselves when attempting to solve problems, while Piaget labelled this behaviour as egocentric and having little relevance to cognitive development, Vygotsky believed that this 'private speech' is an extension of the child's social interaction with others and that they are mimicking verbal instructions, rules and guidance to direct their own behaviour. As the child becomes better at doing this the 'private speech' becomes 'inner speech', an internal language that vastly improves the child's decision making ability.

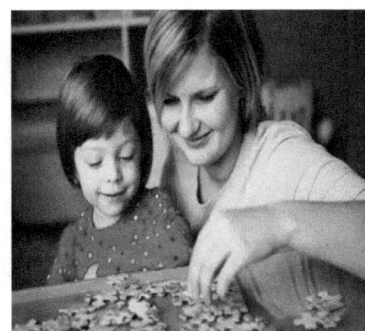

Vygotsky's belief that social processes influence and shape a child's learning and cognitive development is often referred to as sociocultural theory. The main assumption of this theory is that through social interaction children learn how to use cultural tools, such as cutlery or computers, which enables them to develop their own skills and functioning

Explain how Vygotsky's theory of cognitive development supports the nurture debate within psychology.

....

....

....

....

(2 marks)

Let's take a look at the main differences between Vygotsky and Piaget's theories of cognitive development.

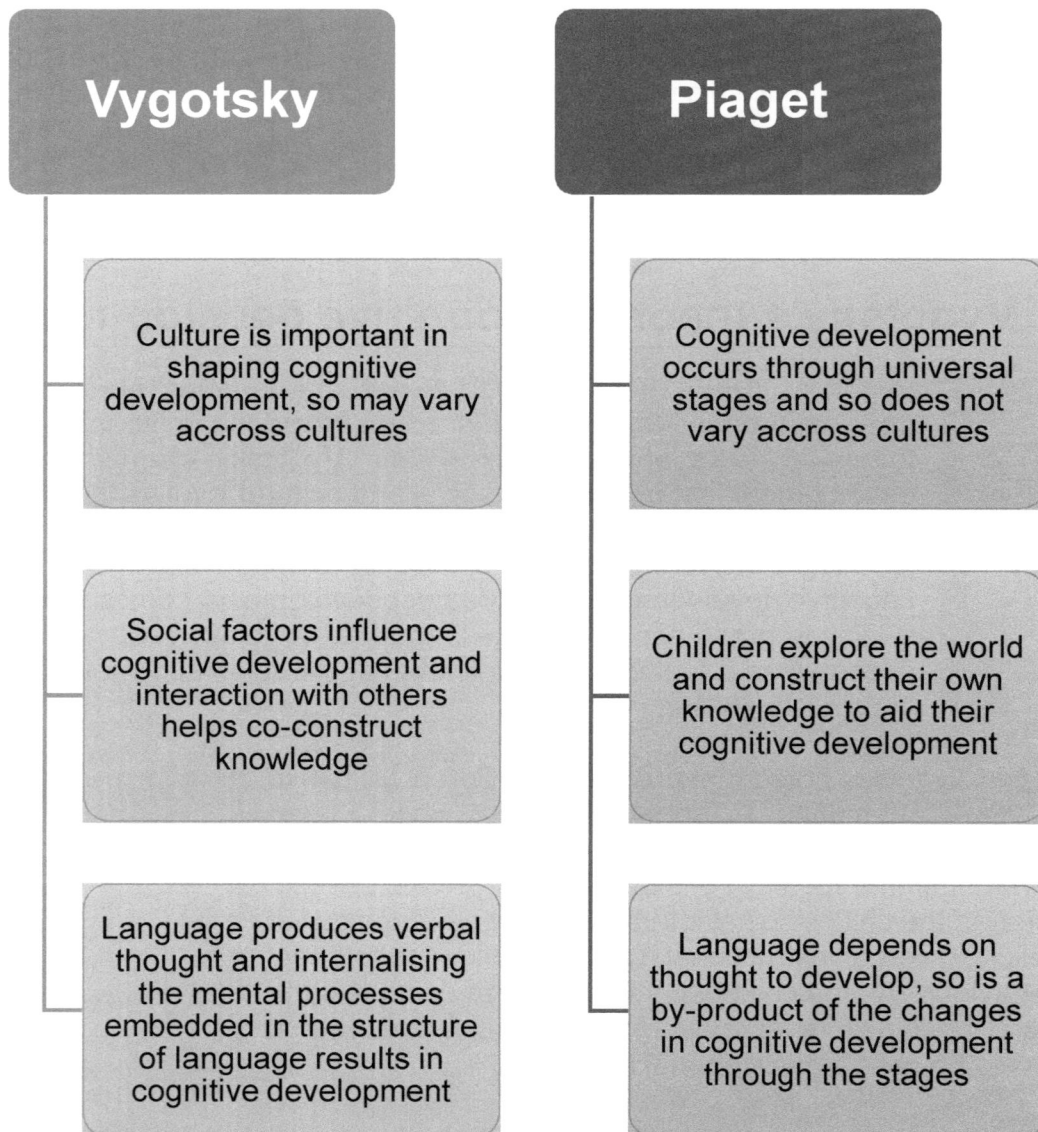

Vygotsky	Piaget
Culture is important in shaping cognitive development, so may vary accross cultures	Cognitive development occurs through universal stages and so does not vary accross cultures
Social factors influence cognitive development and interaction with others helps co-construct knowledge	Children explore the world and construct their own knowledge to aid their cognitive development
Language produces verbal thought and internalising the mental processes embedded in the structure of language results in cognitive development	Language depends on thought to develop, so is a by-product of the changes in cognitive development through the stages

Outline the importance of speech and language in Vygotsky's theory of cognitive development.

....

....

....

....

....

....

....

....

....

(4 marks)

Outline two differences between Vygotsky's theory and Piaget's stage theory of cognitive development.

....

....

....

....

....

....

....

....

....

....

....

(4 marks)

Zone of Proximal Development

Vygotsky believed that cognitive development would develop quicker and that a child would become better at problem solving with the aid of more knowledgeable others, such as parents, teachers, other adults and even peers. He called this the Zone of Proximal Development (ZPD) and it represents the gap between what the child's actual cognitive ability to problem solve on their own and what they can achieve through problem solving with the help of others. Therefore, Vygotsky believed that greater social interaction between the child and others would broaden the child's zone of Proximal Development.

Tasks the child can accomplish on their own

Zone of Proximal Development

A task is too dificult for the child to master on their own, but can be accomplished with guidance and encouragment from a more knowledgeable other

Tasks that are too difficult for the child to accomplish even with help from others

Learning

Vygotsky assumed that cognitive development could be aided by collaboration with others. True or false?

True ☐   False ☐

(1 mark)

Outline what is meant by the term Zone of Proximal Development in Vygotsky's theory of cognitive development.

....

....

....

....

(2 marks)

Research conducted by Gallimore and Tharp (1990) and Tudge (1990) found that social interaction with more knowledgeable others, such as teachers and family members was a critical element of a child's educational growth. This supports Vygotsky's assumption that assistance and guidance in the ZPD aids cognitive development.

Peter is completing his maths homework. He can confidently answer the questions that require addition skills but he is struggling with subtraction. To encourage him, his father sits with him to guide him to the correct answer. The following week Peter is able to complete his maths homework without the help of his father.

Explain how this scenario supports Vygotsky's Zone of Proximal Development.

....

....

....

....

....

....

....

....

....

....

....

....

....

(6 marks)

Scaffolding

Building on Vygotsky's work, research carried out by Wood et al (1976) found that a child working with their mother can achieve better understanding through encouragement, demonstrations, reminders and suggestions. They called this social support 'scaffolding' as the adult's knowledge and guidance acts as a temporary support in the construction of new intellectual levels in the child's cognitive development. Another study by NcNaughton and Leyland (1990) found that children performed better on puzzles when encouraged by mum than when working alone, adding further support for the importance of scaffolding.

Van der Veer (2007) argues that assistance should be given on tasks that are just above the child's capabilities in order to build on their existing knowledge and advance their learning, so scaffolding works best when it is targeted to the needs of the child appropriately. According to Morrissey and Brown (2009) the ultimate aim of scaffolding is the "transfer of responsibility for a task to the child as adult support decreases and child capability increases".

Wood et al (1976) identified that effective instructional scaffolding may involve the following processes:

- **Demonstrating the skills needed to complete a particular task**
- **Maintaining the child's focus and interest in the task**
- **Simplifying the task to make it easier for the child to understand**
- **Providing motivation and encouragement to continue with the task**

Describe what is meant by the term scaffolding in Vygotsky's theory of cognitive development.

....

....

....

....

(2 marks)

Scaffolding is used to provide permanent support for children throughout their cognitive development. True or false?

True ☐   False ☐

(1 mark)

Outline two ways in which an adult can build student skills through scaffolding

....

....

....

....

....

....

....

(4 marks)

Molly is learning to ride her bike but a series of tumbles has knocked her confidence. Her best friend Laura is a confident cyclist so her mum advises her to watch how Laura rides her bike and encourages Molly to continue trying practicing.   Two weeks later, Molly is able to go on a bike ride to the next village with Laura.

Explain how the example above demonstrates the importance of scaffolding in learning.

....

....

....

....

....

....

....

....

....

....

....

(4 marks)

Much of the research supporting Vygotsky's theory of cognitive development use small sample sizes. Outline one problem with drawing conclusions from these studies when looking at cognitive development.

....

....

....

....

....

(2 marks)

Vygotsky's theory is often criticised as it over-emphasises the role of social interaction. Describe one other factor that may explain the rate of cognitive development.

....

....

....

....

....

(2 marks)

Evaluation

Strengths

- Vygotsky's theory has been very influential in developing effective educational practices, such as collaborative learning, peer tutoring and classroom organisation
- This theory has been developed further by other researchers such as Bruner (1971) who have provided strong evidence for Vygotsky's assumptions
- Research by Neitzel and Stright (2003) shows that children do better at school when their parents engage in scaffolding with them

Limitations

- Vygotsky's theory does not explain in precise details which social interactions are most beneficial for cognitive development
- The concepts and ideas described in the theory are not supported by scientific evidence
- Some social interactions may not be beneficial to learning and can actually make it more difficult and frustrating for the child. Durkin (1995) argues that some people may use their knowledge to control and manipulate the other person

Outline and evaluate Vygotsky's theory of cognitive development.

....

....

....

....

....

....

....

....

....

....

....

....

....

....

....

....

....

....

....

....

....

....

....

....

....

....

....

....

....

....

....

....

....

....

....

....

....

....

....

....

....

....

....

....

....

(16 marks)

Baillargeon's explanation of early infant abilities

Learning Objectives

On completion of this section you should be familiar with the following:

1. Baillargeon's explanation of early infant abilities including;
2. Knowledge of the physical world and violation of expectation research

In the previous sections we have looked at the theories of cognitive development proposed by Piaget and Vygotsky. In this section we will discuss the work carried out by the psychologist Renee Baillargeon at The Infant Cognition Laboratory, based at the University of Illinois and consider how the research they have carried out over the last 30 years has shaped our understanding of early infant abilities with specific focus on how they develop knowledge of the physical world and violation of expectation research.

1. Baillargeon's explanation of early infant abilities

The work carried out at The Infant Cognition Laboratory focuses on cognitive development during the first three years of an infant's life, with specific emphasis on how they make sense of the world around them. This is done through studying the infant's ability to establish that there is a causal relationship between events i.e. that one event (the cause) is systematically related to another event (the effect) and alter their behaviour accordingly. This concept is known as causal reasoning and Baillargeon's work focuses on the following four core areas:

Physical Reasoning	• The ability to predict and interpret the outcomes of physical events
Biological Reasoning	• Recognising that humans are different to animals
Psychological Reasoning	• The ability to predict and interpret the actions of others
Sociomoral Reasoning	• Expectations about how people should behave towards others

Describe what is meant by causal reasoning when looking at cognitive development.

....

....

....

....

(2 marks)

Baillargeon and Spelke (1985) argue that infants are born with the ability to perceive and understand objects and events that happen around them and are not greatly influenced by experiences in the world around them.   This is known as the nativist approach and is in contrast to Piaget and Vygotsky's empiricist view that cognitive development is linked to the senses through language and hearing.   The nativist approach believes that psychologists, such as Piaget and Vygotsky underestimated the abilities of infants and that they are actually much more competent than they claim.

Outline the main assumptions of the nativist approach when explaining cognitive development.

....

....

....

....

(2 marks)

Explain how Baillargeon's explanations of early infant abilities are different to those of Vygotsky and Piaget.

....

....

....

....

....

....

....

....

(4 marks)

2. Knowledge of the physical world and violation of expectation research

Baillargeon (1994) argued that Paiget's claim that young infants do not demonstrate an awareness of object permanence during the sensorimotor stage because they lack the necessary internal mental schema was incorrect. According to Baillargeon, infants fail at this task because they are unable to process the action sequence involved in manipulating the object and the fact that infants tend to look more intensely and for longer at objects or events that are unfamiliar to them demonstrates that they do possess knowledge of the physical world around them. To test the assumption that very young infants possess many of the same fundamental ideas and beliefs about objects and events as adults do, Baillargeon and her colleagues developed the violation of expectation method, in which very young infants are presented with the following two tests:

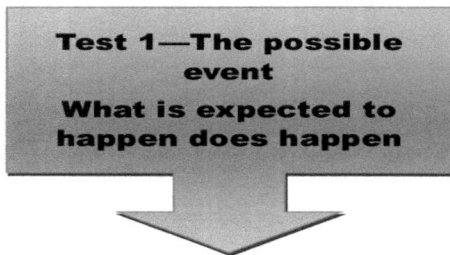

Test 1—The possible event

What is expected to happen does happen

Consistent with expectation

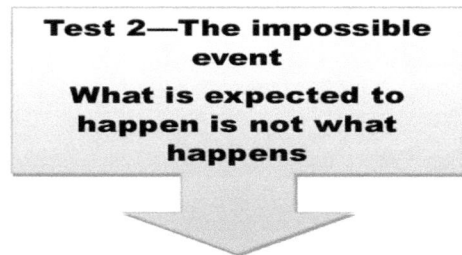

Test 2—The impossible event

What is expected to happen is not what happens

Violation of expectation

Using this experimental method, infants that have been presented with the two tests outlined above, using a variety of different events, have been noted to focus more attention on the impossible event than the possible event. Therefore, supporting the nativist view that young infants have an innate knowledge of the physical world.

Explain what is meant by 'violation of expectation' in relation to Baillargeon's studies of early infant abilities.

....

....

....

....

(2 marks)

Based on the findings of research into violation of expectation, Baillargeon has identified that very young infants form a preliminary concept that captures the overall object or event, but none of the detail. As the infant studies the object or event in more detail they begin to identify variables that relate to it and the effects these variables have on the item. These observations are then incorporated into their reasoning enabling them to make accurate predictions about the outcome of future events. To test this assumption Baillargeon et al (1985) conducted the following study:

Aim

To test the principle that young infants have an awareness of object permanence by seeing if they will study an impossible event for longer than a possible event

Procedure

- 21 American infants aged between 4 and 5 months old
- The infants were placed in front of a screen that was hinged to a table that could be moved back and forth through 180 degrees and were habituated (shown repeatedly) with the movement of the screen
- A box was then placed in the path of the screen and the infants were shown the impossible and possible events
- In the possible event the screen was moved until it came to rest on the box and then it was lowered back to its starting position
- In the impossible event the screen was moved back the full 180 degrees, giving the impression that the box in its path had been flattened
- The length of the infant's gaze was recorded during both events

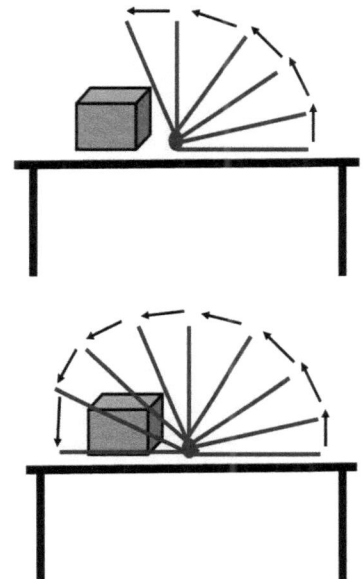

Results

- The infants showed stronger and more consistent interest in the impossible event

Conclusions

- Baillargeon et al concluded that the infants realised that the screen could not move through the space occupied by the box and so understand that objects continue to exist even when they cannot see them

Explain how the findings of Baillargeon et al's (1985) research contradicts Piaget's theory that infants in the sensorimotor stage of cognitive development lack an understanding of object permanence.

....

....

....

....

....

(2 marks)

Baillargeon et al's (1985) research used American infants. Outline the issues that might arise when generalising the findings from this study.

....

....

....

....

....

....

....

....

....

....

(4 marks)

The infants in Baillargeon et al's (1985) study were placed on their mother's knee during the experiment. Outline how this may have influenced the findings of this research.

....

....

....

....

(2 marks)

Further research using violation of expectation tasks carried out by Wang et al (2004) found that even without habituation or familiarisation trials, infants would look at the impossible tasks for longer periods than the possible tasks. In addition, Wilcox et al (1996) carried out a study on 10 week old infants using the violation of expectation method, that involved hiding an object which then reappeared in the same location (possible event) and then in a different location (impossible event). They found that the infants looked longer at the impossible event than the possible event, which provides further support for the nativist assumption that young infants have an innate knowledge of the physical world around them and so demonstrate an understanding about objects and events that Piaget's stage theory claims does not appear until infants are aged 9 to 12 months old.

Briefly outline the method used by Baillargeon to study object permanence.

....

....

....

....

....

....

....

(4 marks)

Evaluation

Strengths

- Many studies that have used Baillargeon's violation of expectation tasks have found evidence for the belief that infants have knowledge of the physical world at a much younger age than claimed by Piaget
- The assumption that young infants have an innate knowledge about objects and events has been adopted by many developmental psychologists and incorporated into theories such as Spelke et al's (1992) core knowledge theory

Limitations

- Psychologists such as Schoner and Thelen (2004) claim that violation of expectation tasks only show us that infants notice a difference between the two events, so argue that Baillargeon may have exaggerated the importance of the findings of her studies
- Haith (1998) argues that there are many reasons why the infants may have looked at the impossible event for longer, such a familiarity or the time lapse between the two events, therefore making it difficult to conclude that their behaviour was down to one particular variable i.e. violation of expectation

Discuss Baillargeon's explanation of early infant abilities.

....

....

....

....

....

....

....

....

....

....

....

....

....

....

....

....

....

....

....

....

....

....

....

....

....

....

....
....
....
....
....
....
....
....
....
....
....
....
....
....
....
....
....
....
....
....
....
....
....

(16 marks)

The Development of Social Cognition

Learning Objectives

On completion of this section you should be familiar with the following:

1. The development of social cognition
2. Selman's levels of perspective-taking
3. Theory of mind, including theory of mind as an explanation for autism; the Sally-Anne study
4. The role of the mirror neuron system in social cognition

In this section we will look at how social psychologists have attempted to explain how we understand and think about people and social situations by examining three theories of social cognition: perspective-taking, theory of mind and mirror neurons.

1. The development of social cognition

Social cognition has its roots in social psychology and is concerned with exploring the way in which people interact with each other and their environment. It studies the individual within a social or cultural context and focuses on how people store and process information and later retrieve and use this information to deal with social situations. This process leads to the development of the individual and a broader understanding of the feelings and thoughts of others. Some of the questions research into social cognition try to answer are:

- How do we work out what other people are thinking or feeling?
- How do our thoughts influence our feelings?
- How do mental processes influence the way form impressions of other people?
- How does the way we view ourselves influence our relationships with others?

By studying children as they grow, developmental psychologists analyse how children and adolescents become aware of their own feelings, thoughts and motives and also how they develop an awareness of the emotions and mental states of others. As this awareness increases, researchers look at how children become more competent at understanding how others are feeling, responding in social situations, engaging in prosocial behaviours, and taking the perspective of others.

Outline what is meant by social cognition.

....

....

....

....

....

(2 marks)

According to some psychologists social cognition is linked to a sense of self and that the development of a sense of self is crucial to having healthy and satisfying relationships as an adult. Kaplan (1978) argues that this sense of self begins from the moment we are born, as a newborn is only aware of their own existence and does not yet understand that the touch and comfort of the mother is from someone separate to themselves. Gradually, the infant becomes aware of their separation from their mother and will begin to develop independence and a sense of self. Striano and Reid (2006) claim that social interaction through eye to eye contact is essential to developing a strong sense of self and that by 3 months of age regular eye to eye contact occurs and by nine months the infant uses is able to direct their gaze to where others are looking or pointing. On an emotional level, developing a sense of self involves learning how to recognise and deal with our own feelings and understanding that others also have feelings that may not be the same as our own. This understanding of feelings allows us to respond appropriately in later social interaction and set boundaries for future relationships and without this personal and emotional sense of self we will not be able to interact successfully with other people.

Explain how sense of self leads to the development of social cognition.

....

....

....

....

....

....

....

....

....

(4 marks)

Meltzoff (1999) claims that social cognition develops through imitation and that by 14 months old, infants are able to remember and repeat actions that they have observed in adults, other children or in the media. Imitation is a powerful way of transmitting appropriate cultural and social behaviour, empathy and moral understanding, which enables us to form meaningful relationships with others. In addition, by imitating behaviour we are also able to understand the intentions of others even if their behaviour does not necessarily produce the correct results. Meltzoff's research found that by 18 months of age, infants generally 'get the gist' of what someone is doing and can understand what was meant to happen.

Social cognition develops through a combination of innate abilities and interaction with the environment. True or false?

True ☐ False ☐

(1 mark)

Imitation allows infants to learn empathy and develop moral understanding. True or false?

True ☐ False ☐

(1 mark)

Explain how imitation leads to the development of social cognition.

....

....

....

....

....

....

....

....

....

....

(4 marks)

2. Selman's levels of perspective-taking

Selman (1974) believed that the development of social cognition and effective social interaction occurs through our ability to understand other people's perspective and that this only develops once we understand our own feelings. As a result, the process of social cognition and develops gradually over many years. By presenting children with social dilemmas and examining their answers, Selman proposed a stage theory, which outlined the development of perspective-taking.

Stage 1 - Undifferentiated perspective-taking (3 to 6 years old)

In this stage children recognise that others can have different thoughts and feelings to them, but they frequently confuse the two

Stage 2 - Social-informational perspective-taking (5 to 9 years old)

Children begin to understand that others may have different perspectives to them as they have access to different information

Stage 3 - Self-reflective perspective-taking (7 to 12 years old)

Children are able to 'step in another person's shoes' and view their own thoughts, feelings, and behaviour from the other person's perspective

Stage 4 - Third-party perspective-taking (10 to 15 years old)

Children are able to step outside a two-person situation and imagine how the self and other are viewed from the point of view of a third, impartial party

Stage 5 - Societal perspective-taking (14 years old to adulthood)

The individual is able to understand that third-party perspective-taking can be influenced by their own personal values and the values of society

Children in Selman's third level of perspective-taking have the ability to see things from another person's viewpoint. True or false?

True ☐   False ☐

(1 mark)

Children in Selman's fourth level of perspective-taking understand that the view of a third party can be influenced by many different factors. True or false?

True ☐ False ☐

(1 mark)

Describe each of the stages outlined in Selman's levels of perspective-taking.

....

....

....

....

....

....

....

....

....

....

....

....

....

....

....

(6 marks)

Let's take a look at the research that supports Selman's levels of perspective-taking:

Gurucharri and Selman (1982)
- Conducted a longitudinal study of 41 American boys
- Found that their role-taking skills improved over a five year period

Yeates et al (1991)
- Found that high scores on social problem-solving tests were positively corralated with better perspective-taking and stronger inter-personal relationships

Burack et al (2006)
- 49 maltreated and 49 demographically matched nonmaltreated children were interviewed to test their levels of perspective-taking
- Concluded that the maltreated children were delayed in their social persepctive-taking development compared to the nonmaltreated children

Selman (2003) argues that interaction between parents, other adults and peers can help children develop perspective-taking skills, therefore improving their social skills and ability to form relationships with others. Fitzgerald and White (2003) found that children with better perspective-taking skills displayed more pro-social behaviours and that children with lower perspective-taking skills were more likely to be aggressive towards their peers. Bolger et al (1998) found that children that had been maltreated were less empathetic than children who had a normal upbringing. They believed that this was a result of their inability to take the perspective of others as a result of observing socially inadequate behaviour in their parents.

Additionally, psychologists such as Keating and Clark (1980) claim that there is a relationship between Selman's levels of perspective-taking and Piaget's stages of cognitive development. They point to the fact that pre-operational children fit into Selman's first stage, concrete operational children are in stages two and three and those who have reached the formal operational stage are in stage four and five of Selman's levels. This supports the idea that the development of social cognition is innate and based on maturation as well as social interaction.

Many of the research studies looking at Selman's levels of perspective-taking have been conducted in America. Outline one issue that might arise when drawing conclusions from these studies.

....

....

....

....

....

(2 marks)

Explain how Selman's levels of perspective-taking is supported by Piaget's stage theory of cognitive development.

....

....

....

....

....

(2 marks)

Selman's research used hypothetical social dilemmas to study perspective-taking. Describe an issue that might arise when using the responses to these dilemmas to explain social cognition.

....

....

....

....

....

(2 marks)

Much of the evidence in support of Selman's levels of perspective-taking is correlational. Outline one strength and one limitation of this research method.

....

....

....

....

....

....

....

....

....

....

(4 marks)

Kurdek (1977) argues that perspective-taking requires complex social skills, which cannot fit neatly in the five stages outlined by Selman. Also, Selman's levels ignore individual differences and the effects these differences might have on their social abilities. Neither does it explain why some children have good abilities in respect of perspective-taking, but are not very adept at social interaction, so perspective taking is not the full story. Additionally, Jarvela and Hakkinen (2003) argue that the levels of perspective-taking cannot explain the new kinds of relationships people have via social media, as they do not follow the normal dynamics of social exchanges. As a result Selman's model may be limited in its use as an explanation of how social cognition develops.

Although there is a great deal of criticism of Selman's levels of perspective-taking, it has been applied successfully to educational practices. Keefe and Johnston (1989) show that teacher who are able to take the emotional perspective of their pupils can modify their teaching style to accommodate their individual needs. In addition, Schonert-Reichl at al (2003) found that when children were encouraged to consider the perspective of others instances of bullying were significantly reduced.

Outline two strengths and two limitations of Selman's levels of perspective-taking.

....

....

....

....

....

....

....

....

....

....

....

....

....

....

(6 marks)

3. Theory of mind

Successful engagement with the social world leads to a child's ability to 'read the minds of others' and to be able to predict the emotions and feelings of others without verbal communication. This deep understanding of others is known as 'Theory of Mind' (ToM). Rendall et al (2000) describes ToM as having "the ability to recognise that others have knowledge, thoughts and feelings apart from their own". That is, we realise that other people also have intentions, knowledge, beliefs and emotions. Most researchers claim that Theory of Mind develops gradually and occurs around 4 years of age.

The term ToM was first used by Woodruff & Premack (1979) who observed that chimpanzees have the ability to intentionally deceive their keepers. Having seen the food being hidden in one of two containers, the chimpanzee indicated to the keeper which container she wanted. One keeper would give her the food in the container, whereas the second keeper would give her the other container. The chimpanzee could discriminate between these two keepers and modified her request to always get the food. Therefore, suggesting that the chimpanzee has the complex ability to be able to predict other people's behaviours based on her own actions.

Explain the problems with drawing conclusions from animal research when looking at the Theory of Mind.

....

....

....

....

(2 marks)

According to Astington and Jenkins (1999) language development is crucial to the development of Theory of Mind and this is supported by research carried out by Lohmann et al (2005), who found that children with better language ability were more proficient at false-belief tasks than those with lower ability. In addition, Baron-Cohen (1995) claims that Theory of Mind is also developed through a shared attention mechanism, where children combine information from their own direction of gaze with that of other people. Once children are able to use this mechanism they can understand that another person can see the same object as they can, and, importantly, that the second person can understand that they can see the object. This is supported by a longitudinal study carried out by Charman et al (2000) that found children who had a lot of shared attention from their parent scored highly on Theory of Mind tasks at 20 months and two year old.

Outline what is meant by the term Theory of Mind.

....

....

....

....

....

(2 marks)

The following research studies support the Theory of Mind:

Onishi & Baillargeon (2005)
- Used non-verbal belief task to examine the ability of 15 month old infants to predict the behaviour of another when a toy has been hidden
- They found that the infants looked longer at the event where the actor did not look for the toy where they believed it should be, so supporting the idea that very young infants have a Theory of Mind

Wellman (2001)
- Conducted a meta-analysis of 178 studies
- Found that all children developed an insight into the beliefs of others between 3 and 5 years old regardless of their cultural and educational background, so Theory of Mind has cross-cultural support

Meins et al (1998)
- Carried out a longitudinal study and concluded that children are able to recognise that other people have alternative perspectives when they are around three and half years old

Many of the false-belief tasks used to test Theory of Mind are very complex. Outline what effect this might have on the findings of this research

....

....

....

....

(2 marks)

Theory of mind as an explanation for autism and the Sally-Anne study

Many psychologists believe that individuals that fail to develop Theory of Mind and a strong sense of self will have serious social problems. Baron-Cohen et al (1985) looked at autistic children who seemed to live in their own little world and showed no regard for the existence of others. They believed that autistic children have not developed a 'Theory of Mind' and therefore do not understand that others have their own thoughts and feelings about the world.

To investigate this, Baron-Cohen (1985) used the Wimmer and Perner (1983) Sally-Anne test, which was designed to test for a child's ability to understand what another person believes and can be easily solved by 'normal' five year olds.

Aim

To test the hypothesis that autistic children with a normal IQ will perform significantly worse on a test that requires them to predict how someone else will behave, than 'normal' children and children with Down's Syndrome

Procedure

- A quasi-experiment using an independent measures design
- Participants:
  20 autistic children, aged between 6 and 16 years old,
  14 Down's Syndrome children, aged between 6 and 17 years old
  27 'normal' children aged between 3 and 5 years old
- The experimenter sits at a table with two dolls, Sally and Anne. Sally puts a marble in her basket and then leaves the play. While Sally in away, Anne takes the marble from the basket and hides it in her box
- Each child is then asked two control questions:
  Where was the marble in the beginning? (The memory question)
  Where is the marble really? (The reality question)
- The child is then asked the critical question:
  When Sally comes back, where will she look for her marble? (The belief question) – if the children point to Anne's box they have failed the belief question as they have not taken Sally's false belief that the marble is still in her basket into account

Results

- All the children in the three groups answered the control questions correctly. On the critical belief question, 85% of the 'normal' children, 86% of the Down's Syndrome children and 20% of the autistic children answered correctly

Identify the naturally occurring independent variable in this experiment.

....

....

(1 mark)

What is the dependent variable in this experiment?

....

....

....

(2 marks)

Identify an appropriate statistical test for this experiment and justify your answer.

....

....

....

....

(3 marks)

Draw a table of results in the space below. Make sure that you provide a suitable title for your table.

(4 marks)

Conclusions

- They concluded that the autistic children could not distinguish between what they believed and what Sally believed; therefore they lacked a theory of mind.

Outline one strength and one limitation of the research methodology used in Baron-Cohen et al's (1985) Sally-Anne study.

....

....

....

....

....

....

....

(4 marks)

Outline one ethical issue that might have arisen during Baron-Cohen et al's (1985) study and explain how the researchers could deal with this issue.

....

....

....

....

(3 marks)

Not all the autistic children in Baron-Cohen et al's (1985) study failed to answer the belief question. What does this tell us about Theory of Mind as an explanation for autism?

....

....

....

....

(2 marks)

Further research by Baron-Cohen and Jolliffe (1997) found that people with autistic spectrum disorders have not developed the ability to interpret the feelings and emotions of others through eye to eye contact in early childhood.

Describe how Baron-Cohen and Jolliffe's (1997) study supports the development of Theory of Mind.

....

....

....

....

(2 marks)

Although Baron-Cohen et al's (1985) study has been significant in stimulating further research into autism there are some that argue that because some autistic individuals consistently pass the false-belief tasks there must be other cognitive impairments that cause autism. Frith and Happe (1994) highlight the fact that autism is not only limited to impairments in the ability to understand what another person believes. So, they proposed the Central Coherence Theory that claims that autism is characterised by an imbalance within the information processing system, which explains why those with autism can often process fixed or clear information easier than information that requires a recognition of its wider meaning.

Siegal and Beattie (1991) also argue that the wording of the critical belief question in Baron-Cohen's (1985) study may have been confusing. Some of the children may have interpreted it to mean "where should Sally look for her marble?" rather than "where will she look for her marble?" This problem was highlighted in research carried out by Saltmarsh, Mitchell and Robinson (1995), who found that differences in the way a task was presented had an impact on whether the children displayed Theory of Mind or not.

Outline how Theory of Mind supports both the nature and nurture debate in psychology.

....

....

....

....

....

....

....

....

(4 marks)

Discuss Theory of Mind as an explanation for autism.

....

....

....

....

....

....

....

....

....

....

....

....

....

....

....

....

....

....

....

....

....

....

....

....

....

....

....

....

....

....

....

....

....

....

....

....

....

....

....

....

....

....

....

(16 marks)

4. The role of the mirror neuron system in social cognition

The stage theories that we have looked at and Theory of Mind can all be criticised for being too simplistic and failing to take into account the individual biological differences that may influence the successful development of the child. In this section we will look at a biological explanation for the development of social cognition, with specific emphasis on the role of the mirror neuron system. Still a young field in this area, social neuroscience is an interdisciplinary approach concerned with looking at how biological systems influence social processes and shape behaviour. A number of methods are used in social neuroscience to investigate the role of neural mechanisms, such as MRI scanning. The research focuses on the brains of 'normal' human participants, known as neurotypicals compared to autistic participants.

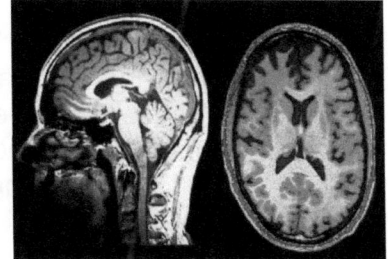

Moll et al (2002) and Amaral et al (2003) have found evidence that the orbitofrontal cortex is involved in social and moral judgments and the amygdala is involved in emotional processing, recognising and interpreting facial emotions. If these areas of the brain are involved in the development of social cognition, research should show differences in these neural structures between neurotypical and autistic participants. Frith (2001) found that the amygdala and the frontal cortex of the autistic participants were abnormal, which may explain why the autistic participants in the earlier research on ToM had problems interpreting facial expressions.

Outline the main assumptions of the biological approach in psychology.

....

....

....

....

(2 marks)

Describe how social neuroscience methods have been used to explain the development of social cognition.

....

....

....

....

(2 marks)

Although these explanations provide a neurological cause for problems with social cognition, they do not explain why these abnormalities may have occurred. Many researchers claim that such abnormalities are hereditary and therefore, problems with social cognition have a genetic basis. If this is true then we would expect to find a high concordance in social cognition problems between family members. This genetic assumption is supported by a large volume of research into monozygotic (MZ) and dizygotic (DZ) twins, which have shown extremely high concordance rates up to 90% of both twins having autism.

One of the most important discoveries into the biological explanations of social cognition is the firing of mirror neurons that has been observed in the frontal lobes of macaque monkeys. Research by Di Pellegrino et al (1992) looked at the brain images of the monkeys and found that the mirror neurons fired when the monkeys are performing a specific task are the same mirror neurons that fire in the brains of the monkeys that are observing the task.

Explain why it is difficult to generalise the findings from animal studies looking at the development of social cognition.

....

....

....

....

(2 marks)

Rizzolatti et al (2006) discovered that when humans observe others in pain, the same areas of the brain are active as when we are in pain ourselves. So, our neurons are mirroring what we have observed, helping us to feel empathy with the other person. Mukamel et al (2010) argue that this 'mirroring' is the neural mechanism by which the actions, intentions and emotions of other people can be automatically understood and is the foundation of empathy.

Indirect research by Dapretto and Cox (2007) used MRI scanning to look at the area of the brain in 'normal' and autistic children, believed to be associated with mirror neuron activity as indentified by the earlier monkey research. They found that activity in this area was significantly less in the autistic children than in the 'normal' children. They concluded that these differences in their neuro-anatomy prevented imitative behaviour and the ability to empathise with others, leading to problems in the development of social cognition. These findings are also supported by Oberman et al (2003) and Gazzola et al (2006), who found that individuals who score low on measurers of empathy and those who are autistic have less activity in the area associated with mirror neuron activity.

One of the functions of mirror neurons is to facilitate the understanding of others' feelings and actions. True or false?

True [ ]　False [ ]

(1 mark)

Explain how the mirror neuron explanation for the development of social cognition can be described as reductionist.

....

....

....

....

(2 marks)

Research has shown a relationship between an impairment in the functioning of the mirror neuron system. Explain the limitation of using these findings when explaining the role of mirror neurons in social cognition.

....

....

....

....

(2 marks)

Social cognition is a very broad area. Outline why this makes it difficult to generalise the findings from research into the role of mirror neurons.

....

....

....

....

(2 marks)

Although there is still a great deal of research to be done in this field of study, it is clear that the biological contribution has enhanced our understanding of social cognition and the discovery of underlying genetic and biological factors that affect our ability to develop a sense of self, Theory of Mind and perspective-taking is helping us to better understand autism. However, there are many features of autism that none of these theories can adequately explain, such as obsessional behaviour, the intolerance of change and certain language deficits. As technology and scientific methods become more sophisticated, the work already carried out on the mirror neuron system will no doubt pave the way for exciting new research that underpins and complements the work on the psychological processes that enable us to interact socially and understand others.

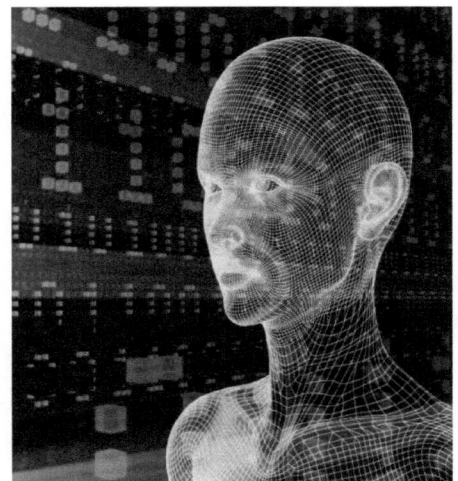

Describe and evaluate one or more theories that seek to explain the development of social cognition.

....

....

....

....

....

....

....

....

....

....

....

....

....

....

....

....

....

....

....

....

....

....

....

....

(16 marks)

L - #0438 - 171120 - C0 - 297/210/6 - PB - DID2952581